GARDENS of the
ITALIAN LAKES

GARDENS
of the

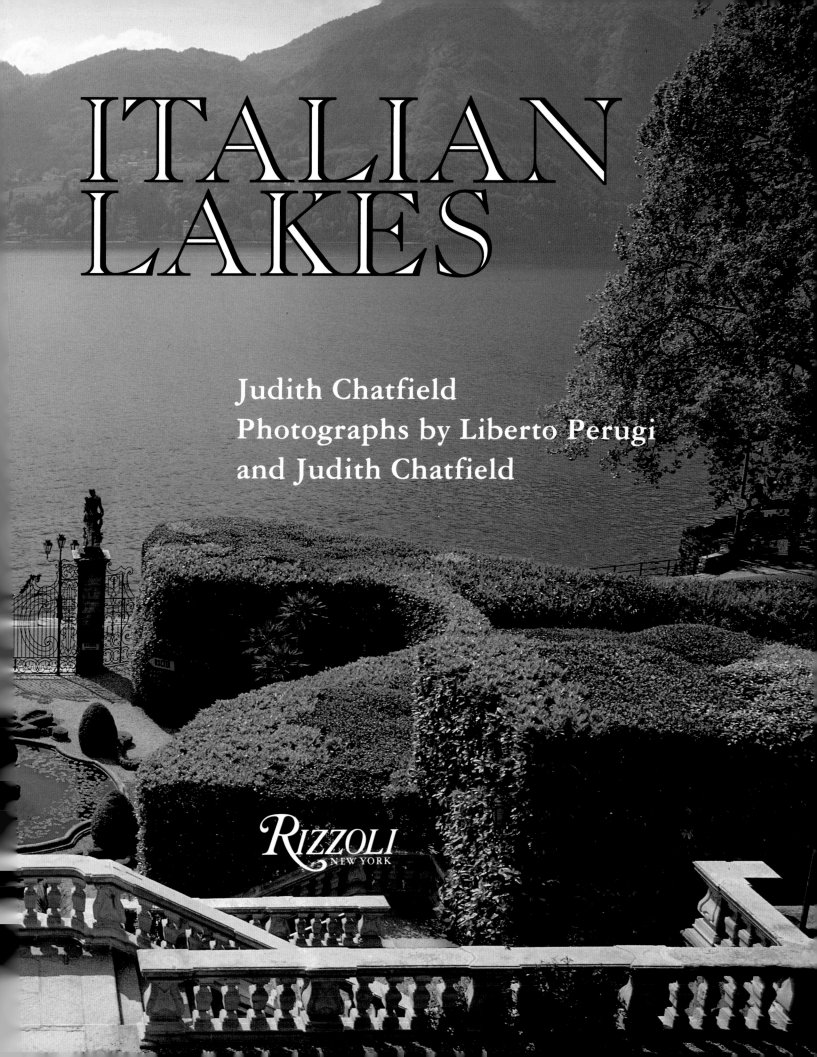

ITALIAN LAKES

Judith Chatfield
Photographs by Liberto Perugi
and Judith Chatfield

RIZZOLI
NEW YORK

First published in the United States of America in 1992 by
RIZZOLI INTERNATIONAL PUBLICATIONS, INC.
300 Park Avenue South, New York, New York 10010

Library of Congress Cataloging-in-Publication Data

Chatfield, Judith.
    Gardens of the Italian lakes/ Judith Chatfield: photographs
by Liberto Perugi and Judith Chatfield.
    Includes index and bibliography.
    ISBN 0–8478–1601–X
    1. Gardens—Italy.   2. Gardens—Italy—Pictorial
works. 3   Lakes—Italy.   4. Lakes—Italy—Pictorial
works.   I. Title.
SB466.I8C418 1992
712'.6'09452—dc20   92–8182
                                     CIP

Designed by Mary McBride
Printed and bound by Cromolito in Italy

TITLE PAGE: Villa Carlotta
COPYRIGHT PAGE: Engraving of Villa Carlotta by Wetzel
PART TITLE: page 17: Grand Hotel Villa Serbelloni

Contents

Map

SWITZERLAND

PIEDMONT

Lake Maggiore

Pallanza • • Verbania

Isola dei Pescatori •
Stresa • • Cerro

Monte Mottarone • Isola Bella

Isola Madre

Lake Lugano

Varese •

Arona •

Lake Como

Grandola • Menaggio •

Griante • • Varenna

Cadenabbia
Tremezzo • Bellagio
Lenno • San Giovanni
Ossuccio →

COMO LECCO

• Nesso

Moltrasio • Lecco
Cernobbio • Torno
Borgovico • • Como

LOMBARDY

ADDA

ITALY

• MILAN

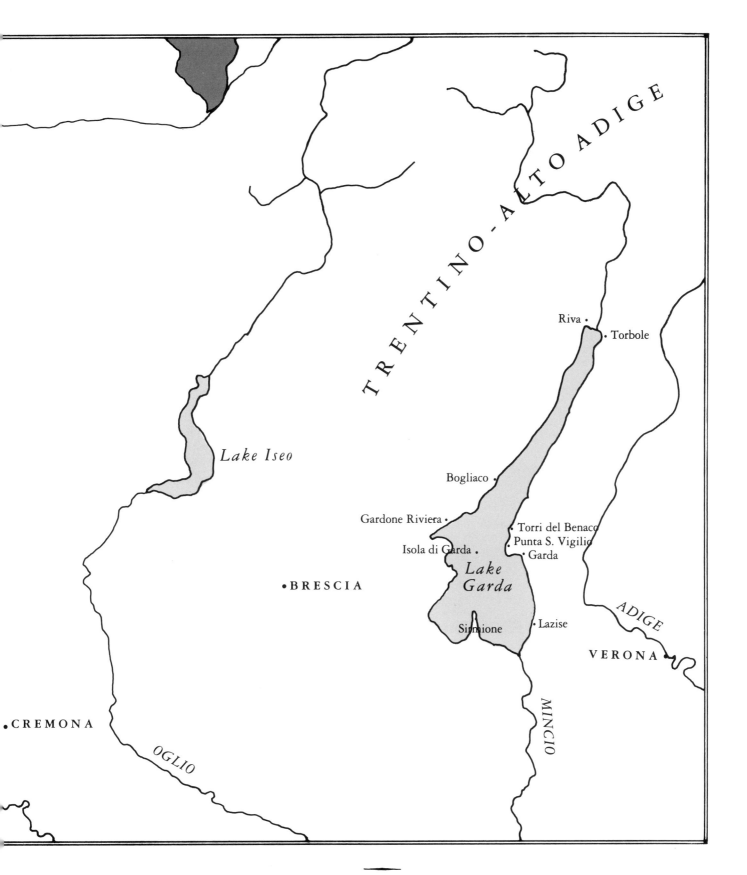

TRENTINO-ALTO ADIGE

Riva •
• Torbole

Lake Iseo

Bogliaco •

Gardone Riviera •
• Torri del Benaco
• Punta S. Vigilio
Isola di Garda •
• Garda

Lake Garda

• BRESCIA

Sirmione
• Lazise

ADIGE

VERONA •

MINCIO

• CREMONA

OGLIO

Statue from Villa Vigoni

INTRODUCTION

"NOTHING IN THE WORLD," wrote Stendhal in 1817, "can be compared to the fascination of those burning summer days passed on the Milanese lakes, in the middle of those chestnut groves so green that they immerse their branches in the waves. . . ."

The great lakes of northern Italy are among the loveliest of European settings. The villas built along their shores or on their islands have served as fashionable seasonal dwellings, or *villegiature*, for generation of Italians and have drawn travelers from around the world.

Each of the lakes has a very distinct character—Maggiore is a lake of passage and a great deal of traffic rolls along the narrow roads, through the towns established for visitors; once there, you abandon your car, thankfully, and board ferryboats that chug from shore to island to island, Isola Bella, to Stresa, Isola Madre to Baveno, and, most enticing of all, Isola dei Pescatori—without a garden but with magical views of the other Borromean islands, Bella and Madre, their gardens slumbering, emptied of tourists at dusk. On Maggiore, too, is Italy's most important botanical garden, Villa Taranto, as well as one of the most visited Baroque gardens in the country—Isola Bella.

Lake Como is stately, the most beautiful villas, still maintained in high style, touch its shores; "It is exagger-

ated to say palaces," wrote Stendhal, "and too understated to call them country houses. There is a style of construction peculiar to the three lakes and the Brianza hills, which is elegant, picturesque, and voluptuous." Fishing villages are tucked in here and there as contrast, once only accessible by boat. The villages appear tailored for an operetta. From such a village one takes a small launch to visit the gardens of Villa Balbianello. The grandest of grand hotels is the former Villa d'Este, its spectacular water theater retained intact from the Renaissance, the rest of the garden married to nineteenth-century romanticism.

Lake Garda is studded with castles. It is a lake of rugged beauty, with shallow marshy shores and cliffs plunging down into deep waters. Parts of it have an Austrian heritage. The western shore road snakes through tunnels, slices between Villa Bettoni and its garden, and winds up to the eccentric dwelling of Gabriele D'Annunzio. The base of the lake is dominated by the busy peninsula of Sirmione, abustle with pedestrians visiting the spa, Roman ruins, and Scaligeri castle. Its eastern shore has the enchanting Punta San Vigilio with its miniscule port, stately cypresses, and olive groves.

This book is directed towards these three lakes—Como, Maggiore, and Garda. Unfair, one might say, to

Lecco, Orta, Lugano, or Iseo. Lecco is the long right arm of Como, hidden behind the promontory of Bellagio. Its western shore is rugged, with a small number of houses, its eastern shore is largely industrial—there are, therefore, few gardens here. Lugano is richer, but most of it is in Swiss territory and hence beyond the scope of this book. Much of Iseo's western and northern shoreline consists of sheer cliffs, descending into the water. Iseo, like Lecco, is somewhat industrial, the source of the famed motorboat building, among other works. As for Orta, it is a small lake, a peaceful spot, but one that has never been as fashionable as Como or Maggiore, and few villas of any size were erected here; as a result, it is not a lake to search out remarkable gardens.

But all of the lakes have in common great natural beauty—the Alps bordering their northern reaches, the sunlight glowing on their western shores in the afternoon, and the blue-green waters lapping pebbled shores.

The water is blue because of its purity, greenish where algae is present. Como and Maggiore are both exceedingly deep lakes, over 1200 feet below sea level. The shallow pebbled shores are transparent. Although Garda is so broad as to appear to be a small sea at the lower half, there are no tides or muddy shorelines. The lakes, alas, are not totally immune to pollution. There are industrial fumes hailing from nearby cities, which create a haze, obscuring the views surrounding the lakes, but when this lifts, you are tempted to plant yourself and gaze for hours at the steep hills, the white-capped Alps to the far north, the masses of deep greens punctuated by tiny villages. Out of the morning haze the eastern shore is the first to light up with the sun's rays. The noonday light is fierce, but the western shores are bathed with golden color in the afternoon—perhaps for this reason, so many of the loveliest villas are sited on the western shores. Then, as the sun sets off the quay at Orta, one can watch the lights appear one by one on the tiny island of San Giulio opposite, or from the Borromean islands, Isola Madre, shrouded in darkness, looming silently over the water.

The character of the gardens of these lakes is unlike any found elsewhere in the country. It should be remembered that most of their villas were built as seasonal dwellings and the plantings followed this concept. Evergreens found in such predominance in Tuscany are not the rule here, for the winter appearance of the garden was not considered. Spring is glorious, with lusher displays of rhododendrons, azaleas, and camellias than found in Eng-

Plan of Isola Madre, from Triggs, Art of Garden Design, *1906.*

land. Some of the gardens, such as Villa Carlotta and Isola Madre, are famed for their spring appearances. Summer flowers are richer in variety than in the southern, drier parts of Italy. Alpine flowers are often cultivated on the lakes. Autumn brings limpid atmosphere and vivid foliage of deciduous trees. Also, it is worthwhile noting that originally, most of the villas were only accessible by water. Roads were put in bordering the shores only much later, and as a result, many gardens were cut off from their landing steps, changing the overall culminating effect of villa and garden. (Villas Carlotta and Sola are victims of road construction.) The rugged terrain, which descends often steeply to the water below, has also contributed to the unique nature of the gardens, giving them a rather eccentric look, as Isola Bella, which rises eerily from the morning mists like a ghost ship. The limited space and uneven terrain has excluded the classic Italian Garden plan of the Renaissance. Gardens on the lakes are positioned where space is available, often terraced to take advantage of spectacular views of the lakes and surrounding mountains. Many of the existent gardens date from the nineteenth century, when the fashion for the English romantic landscape garden style prevailed—re-interpreted to the uneven landscape. This coincided with the importation of many plants from the Far East, and the craze for collections of plant "exotics."

Statue from Villa Carlotta

The who's who of the Italian lakes spans centuries. Dating from ancient Roman settlements, notable personages have settled and sojourned here. Pliny the younger had several residences on Lake Como, one on the promontory of Bellagio, site of Villa Serbelloni today, and another further south at Torno, where the spring still flows intermittently, as in his day. Cattulus loved Lake Garda; on it are the remains of a Roman villa at Sirmione. The early missionary, Julius, preached on Lake Orta. San Carlo Borromeo was born at Arona on Maggiore.

Writers of some of Italy's finest novels made their homes on the lakes. Alessandro Manzoni, author of *I Promessi sposi*, lived at Lecco, and on the shores of Lake Lugano at Oria, the villa of Antonio Fogazzaro, writer of *Piccolo mondo antico,* still stands today. Scenes from these novels vividly depict life on the lakes in the early seventeenth and nineteenth centuries.

In the days before the airplane and big ocean liners, most visitors to Italy crossed the Alps passing one of the large lakes: Maggiore to the west, reached by the St. Gotthard Pass; Como in the center, near to Milan, and Lake Garda, gateway from Austria. The travel memoirs of Goethe and Ruskin are replete with entries about the lakes. The region also had its share of royal visitors, including Queen Caroline of Brunswick, who lived at Villa d'Este on Como, exiled from England by her husband George III. Napoleon and Josephine were fêted on the Borromean islands of Maggiore.

In the sixteenth century, painters Bernardino Luini and Gaudenzio Ferrari adorned the lake churches of Como and Maggiore. Antonio Canova and Bertel Thorwaldsen filled the villas on Lake Como with their neoclassical sculpture in the nineteenth century. Turner painted Lake Maggiore, albeit with artistic license in depicting the surrounding mountains. There are countless watercolors, lovingly executed by foreign visitors around the turn of the century—even without artistic fantasy one cannot help but paint a picturesque view at every turning. The lakes themselves always hold center stage—no matter that the villa is architecturally pleasing, the flowers abundant, the balustrades and steps delightful, one's eyes always return to the lake and the play of the light over its surface.

Life was not always easy on the lakes; they were border crossroads for marauding armies. The number of ruined forts testify to the necessity of generations to be on the *qui vive.* The Romans established military camps along the shores at Sirmione and Como. The lakes saw battle fleets, especially on Como; the cities of Como and Lecco at odds; the Tre Pievi (three medieval towns of Dongo, Gravedona, and Sorico on Como) against the Milanesi who counted Como as their ally. Barbarossa's troops besieged the island of Comacina, forcing its inhabitants to flee and resettle on northern shores, especially Varenna. He got his comeuppance when the Tre Pievi banded together to plunder Barbarossa's rich luggage trains.

The lakes have been dominated over the centuries by the Lombards, followed by the Visconti and Sforza families. They have been stages for political maneuvering—in the late eighteenth century resistance to Austrian domination, in the nineteenth century to French control, and in this century to partisan operations. In the nineteenth century, the lakes were often centers of sedition, the villas hiding political refugees on their way out of the country. Countless plots against the Austrians and French were hatched strolling through garden paths or under shady belvederes. Chapters of Italian independence were plotted and fought out here by Mazzini, Garibaldi, and Cavour. More drama ensued under the Fascist era with Gabriele D'Annunzio sending forth messages from Il Vittoriale. On the western shores of Garda, Benito Mussolini and his mistress Clara Petacci had their residences during the short lived Republic of Salò. Lake Como saw the final hours of Fascism at Dongo where Mussolini's convoy, attempting to flee Italy for Switzerland and safety, was halted and his cohorts summarily tried at the town hall and shot. Mussolini and Petacci's execution was delayed a day and carried out at nearby Azzano. They had not time, nor perhaps the inclination, to cultivate their gardens—Mussolini's was a large wooded park equipped with escape tunnels.

So often on the lakes, especially Como, one encounters a nineteenth-century streak of Romantic morbidity—family mausoleums are tucked into corners of the gardens at Carlotta, Melzi, Vigoni, Pizzo, and Puncia. Houses remain closed for *lustri,* intact at the death of a beloved family member, and columns were erected to remind future generations of the plague. One's first image of the lake district is *ridente*—smiling, sunny, joyous, but when the winds whip up unexpectedly and race down the otherwise protective mountains, there are periods of gray, rainy days, and dampness conducive to melancholy.

Small Romanesque churches along the shores and up on the hills are witnesses to the faith in times of strife. There are beautiful secluded monasteries, such as Piona on Como and Santa Caterina del Sasso on Maggiore; Saint Francis established a community on Isola del Garda, which later became an important seminary under Lecchi. Maggiore is permeated with the memory of its local princely saint, San Carlo Borromeo. A reformed "sinner," he then judged harshly those who did not adhere strictly to the mother church. His inquisition courts held in Como and Dongo sent thousands to *inferno*. But in fairness, it must be said that this man performed acts of great charity as archbishop of Milan during the plague. The worldliness of the Borromeo family is set forth by the scale of their gardens at Isola Bella, terraced rigidly and ornately ever upwards, with the ironic family motto *Humilitas* picked out in flower bedding. The colossal statue of Carlo Borromeo at Arona has this same stroke of pomposity—with effort, one can climb inside the interior to peer out at the lake through the saint's nostrils—but the view is rather unsatisfying.

Lake transportation has considerably improved over the years. The first public ferry on Lake Maggiore began service in 1824. From the foot of the lake at Arona, it chugged up north one day, and made the return trip the following day. On Sunday it rested. Traversing wide distances on the larger lakes had its hazards. Today, travel is much more frequent and safer, but storms still spring up at a moments notice. Suddenly, the far shore is invisible as a dark rain cloud curtain lowers, and the lakes' surfaces become turbulent.

The mountains surrounding Como, Maggiore, and Garda keep the outside world at bay. They embrace and shelter the waters, setting them off as a jeweler would set important sapphires. On Como and once you reach the northern portions of Maggiore and Garda, you feel the separateness of the lakes from the rest of the busy hustling plains of northern Italy. Villages and towns are small, originally settled by fishermen, boatmen, and farmers. Fortunately, there are few ultra modern hotels and much of the area is protected from development. The difficulty of large-scale transportation has retarded growth over the centuries. Much of what we see in villa architecture dates from after the mid-nineteenth century when the ruling house of Savoy made Maggiore and Como fashionable; courtiers followed their lead. Time is arrested on the Italian lakes. The tone there is still that of the nineteenth century today, locked in a time capsule.

THE LAKES

LAKE COMO

OR SHEER ELEGANCE, Lake Como is the queen of the northern lakes. The grand hotels of Villa d'Este and Serbelloni are matchless. The surrounding mountains embrace the entire lake, which is shaped like an inverted Y, with the peninsula of Bellagio dividing the Como and Lecco branches.

Lake Como lies completely in Italian territory, unlike the other lakes, which have portions allotted to Switzerland. It is easily accessible to Milan, just an hour's drive to the south, and has traditionally been a favorite location for a second home for the Milanese. Beautiful villas abound on the Como branch of the lake.

While Lake Como is magnificent in its grandeur, much of its charm derives from its fishing villages, tucked against the hillsides. Occasionally, all the buildings of these villages are putty-colored, but more often they are a potpourri of pastel shades, ochre, rose, russet, and buff. Sheep still graze on the chestnut- and oak-covered slopes.

By early May, Lake Como is in full gear. The first big wave of visitors arrive to view the azaleas and rhododendrons at Villa Carlotta and Villa Melzi. The air is limpid, but snow caps the distant mountains to the north.

Summer brings the part-time residents. Families return to the villas owned by their ancestors for generations; shutters open and voices echo across the water. Water traffic is at its peak—silent sailboats and high-powered speedboats ply the lake—and the roads are thick with congestion. Gardens shimmer in the heat, and drought conditions may set in. By September the lake is still active, but the crowds are thinning out. The gardens are at

ABOVE: *Villa Pliniana in an engraving by Wetzel, 1822.*
RIGHT: *The Romanesque church of Sant'Agata, Moltrasio.*

Goats grazing near the Abbey of Piona.

their lushest. The days are comfortably warm, but by October the weather is unsettled. Toward the end of the month heavy rains bring the lake level up from the three-foot drop in summer drought to a point that necessitates preventive sandbagging at Como's port. The freight and passenger *traghetti* continue their scheduled runs, crisscrossing the lake. In the last week of October, there is a final gasp of tourism, evident by the occasional gap in the rows of room keys hanging in hotel lobbies; but most of the hoteliers begin to close their shutters.

Now, at Bellagio, the clientele of the Cafe Rossi is made up of locals who linger, chatting. At seven A.M. one hears the gentle lapping of water on the shore, and the earliest *traghetto* departs with its headlights on. A full moon still hovers to the west, streaking the pearly gray lake waters. Across the shore at Menaggio and Cadenabbia lights glimmer. By noon, a few tourists are strolling around Villa Melzi's quiet gardens; a Landseer Newfoundland dog waits patiently while her owner sits reading a novel in the sun. On the gravel paths of the garden of Grand Hotel Villa Serbelloni, oriental carpets are spread out to air.

Later in the evening, we head off to a nearby restaurant, and find we are the only customers, but the young hosts put forth their best efforts, pressing upon us the local cake, soaked with hot milk, after we have had our desserts. The leaves are beginning to fall, the air is crisp and marigolds have been touched by frost. In places, pansies have been planted for winter bedding, but most gardens are trimmed and allowed to slumber through the winter months. A few villa owners will return for the Christmas/New Year's holidays, but most will not see their gardens again until spring. It is sunny, but with a golden autumnal haze; far shores and mountains are vaguely visible; western villages are cast in shadows by early afternoon. Villa la Pliniana, site of Pliny the Younger's intermittent spring, never sees the sun. It is still possible to eat out in a sunny piazza at Lenno and shed jackets, but the moment you move into the shade you shiver. It takes endurance to sit out on the deck on the afternoon boat to Como. Yet on the peaceful, late autumn lake you are more apt to hear the squawk of a duck than the buzz of a motorboat. The haze blends the pastel pinks and

LEFT: *A street tabernacle in Menaggio.* FOLLOWING: *The village of Nesso.*
ABOVE: *A glimpse of Varenna.*

ochers of the village buildings.

Lake Como's history is bound up in its boats. The *comballo* was a long barge with towering sails. Better known is the *lucia*, the traditional small, maneuverable fishing boat with wooden ribbing for a protective canvas in rainy weather. Little fishing is done commercially now; fish hatcheries supply the restaurants. The average visitor is now apt to travel by *traghetto*, the ungainly boxy car ferry, or by passenger boat, the normal bus-like ferries, the rapid *aliscafi* (hydrofoils), or the special cruise boats for all day outings—one still steam-powered. Lake Como's first steamboats appeared in 1824, in an era when most villages were accessible only by water or by mule track. Caroline of Brunswick, between 1815 and 1821, ordered the construction of the Via Regina, which linked Como with towns on the western shore, permitting carriage traffic. This spurred the building of villas and hotels.

The earliest formal garden on Lake Como was created late in the sixteenth century by Ercole Sfondrati for his wife at Villa Capuana. This garden, which no longer exists, was described in 1629 by Luigi Rusca. There were lemon and espaliered apple trees, arbors with vines, roses, and jasmine, and neatly trimmed bushes and hedges of laurel and boxwood, as well as cypress trees. Filippo Meda described its cypresses and perfumed *Olea fragrans* blooming in September, the juniper, larch, oak, chestnut, and immemorial olive trees. He wrote of sunbathed stone walls hidden by pear trees, quinces, and pomegranates. Garden paths were traced in ordered fashion, flanked by roses, fruit trees, and tasty capers. Roses and citruses were grown in movable terracotta pots.

As at Lake Maggiore, many of the villas built in the latter part of the nineteenth century follow the fashion for the English landscape park garden.

One cannot fail to share Flaubert's sentiment about Lake Como: "There are some spots on earth which one longs to clasp to one's bosom."

LEFT: *The lakeside facade.*
ABOVE: *A three-hundred year old pine frames the* tempietto.

Villa dell'Olmo
Borgovico

*T*HE NAME OF this villa, *olmo*, or elm, is borrowed from a previous structure existing in the seventeenth century, a guesthouse belonging to a monastery of the Osservanti order. Yet the elms have a still older provenance, described in the writings of Pliny the Younger, who often visited a poet friend, Caninio Rufo, at his villa set in a forest of elms here on Como's shore.

In 1664, Marco Plinio Odescalchi traded two buildings to the monks for this property. His descendant, the Marquis Innocenzo Odescalchi built the grandiose villa between 1782 and 1790 to the designs of architects Innocenzo Ragazzoni and Simone Cantoni. Villa dell'Olmo has always had a distinguished guest list. Napoleon and Josephine Bonaparte stayed here together in 1797, Josephine returning alone in 1805. It also hosted the queens of Sicily and Sardinia in 1835, and the Austrian Emperor Ferdinand I in 1838 under the next owner, the Marquis Giorgio Raimondi.

Raimondi inherited the villa in 1824 through the female line of the Odescalchi. Although he hosted the emperor, Prince Metternich, and Marshall Radetzky for two days with great pomp, Raimondi was actually a rebel against the Austrian domination. He was forced to flee in 1848 to Switzerland, and his villa was comman-

ABOVE: *The formal garden edged by topiary.*
RIGHT: *An arched passageway links the English landscape garden to the formal lakeside garden.*

FOLLOWING: *A statue of an ancient god presides over the formal garden.*

deered as a barracks. Upon his return to Villa dell'Olmo in 1859, he introduced Giuseppe Garibaldi to Giuseppina Raimondi; the two were later married.

The garden as we see it dates from the next owner, Duke Guido Visconti di Modrone. In 1883, he pulled down the wings of the villa and created the forecourt as a formal garden facing the lake. Rectangular flowerbeds set in lawns stretch across the broad terrace. Roses and white geraniums are planted in this terrace garden. In front of the villa, within a clipped box hedge on a lawn, is a large basin with a fountain of over-lifesize tumbling putti sculpted by Oldofredi. On the rim of the basin are sculpted the rather gruesome coats of arms of the Visconti di

Modrone family—a serpent swallowing a child. Statues of gods and goddesses on high pedestals line the gravel walks. A graceful port adjoins the terrace. To the right, by the wrought-iron entrance gate, is a monument to Achille Grandi, a labor leader. To the rear of the villa is a landscaped park with specimen trees, including a Dutch pine, about three hundred years old, and a large chestnut tree. There are still elms in the park where the poet Ugo Foscolo often sat. A graceful marble *tempietto* (or little temple) with a lead roof stands on the hillside.

The villa was given to the city of Como by the heirs of Duke Guido in 1926. It is used for conferences and exhibitions.

Villa Erba
between Como and Cernobbio

*T*HE TOWERING TREES are the true protagonists of
this garden. The late afternoon sun extends their
shadows and sends them streaking across the vast expanses
of emerald lawn. There is a strange, pompous atmosphere
about this overblown, art-nouveau villa—from the surrounding lifesize statuary of mythological figures who
writhe and posture, to the enormous new exhibition hall,
designed by Mario Bellini to resemble greenhouses. This is
a superb landscape park: all the carefully grouped trees are
deciduous, including groves of bamboo and purple beech. A
grouping of enormous plane trees shades a small raised terrace, bordered by white pansies. The long curving shoreline
is lushly planted with white roses. In front of the villa's
steps, a private rustic port has been excavated; its rough
boulders are echoed by clipped box behind them. These artificial, manmade elements intermixed with natural ones is
typical of the art nouveau garden of this period.

The villa was conceived around 1892 for the art collector and musician Luigi Erba who was heir to a pharma-
ceutical company fortune. In the early nineteenth century,
the Napoleonic general Pino had transformed an old con-
vent into a villa. This stood next to Erba's villa. The current
owners, Visconti di Modrone, operate the estate as a conference center.

31

LEFT: *White pansies encircle a shaded terrace.*
ABOVE: *Greenhouse-like exhibition hall by Mario Bellini.*

Grand Hotel Villa d'Este

Cernobbio

LEFT: *The* nymphaeum *frames the cypress allée.*
ABOVE: *Twin water staircases.*

*T*HE MOST SPLENDID Baroque garden on Lake Como is undoubtedly that of the Grand Hotel Villa d'Este. Even in its fragmented state, the *nymphaeum* and cypress allée are majestic. Gone now are the complex parterres that formerly existed; yet the detail of the pebble-faced *nymphaeum*, with its niches and chambers, has a richness that was once echoed in the old parterres beneath it. Between the two wings is an oval court decorated with bas-reliefs, caryatides, and a pool. In the center of the cypress allée, a trickling water staircase descends from a niche at the summit. Decorated in a fashion similar to the *nymphaeum*, it contains a marble statue of Hercules. By the water's edge is a later *tempietto*, sheltering a statue of Minerva before a bust of Telemachus.

The villa was originally built by Pellegrino Pellegrini sometime between 1568 and 1615 for Cardinal Tolomeo Gallio. Born to a local fisherman, Gallio owned a series of princely villas along Como's shores, including residences at Gravedona and Ossuccio.

The *nymphaeum* can be safely attributed to Pellegrini. Gallio's nephew inherited it and passed it on to the Jesuits, who rented it out after 1769. Eventually, it was purchased for the former ballerina, "La Pelusina," by her

ABOVE: *Caryatides surround a small pond within the nymphaeum.*   FOLLOWING: *A blaze of begonias by the waterfront.*

first husband, the Marquis Bartolomeo Calderara. In honor of her second husband's military career (General Domineco Pino waged a campaign for Napoleon in Spain), she landscaped the steep hillside behind the garden with miniature forts. After it had suffered years of neglect, La Pelusina restored and improved the lovely property.

The Villa d'Este had its most colorful period during the five-year ownership of Queen Caroline of Brunswick, wife of King George IV of England. Estranged from her husband, she lived here with her lover and high chamberlain, Bartolomeo Bergami, between 1815 and 1820, before returning to England for her divorce trial. Villa d'Este received its name from her ancestor, Guelfo d'Este. Queen Caroline set up a miniature court here and conducted one

lavish entertainment after another. For the villa's housewarming, the court singer Bernardo Bellini sang:

> "Where the Lario, laughing
> A mirror makes so rare
> of Pliny's happy love-nest,
> Dear to Love and Venus fair,
> and Aurora comes murmuring
> His welcome to the pair"
> (Batcheller, *Italian Castles and Country Seats*, 1911).

The Baron Ippolito Gaetano Ciani acquired Villa d'Este in 1820. It became the setting for a patriotic ball celebrating Italian unification in 1861. Triumphal arches of laurel and oak decorated the garden where the dances were held. The

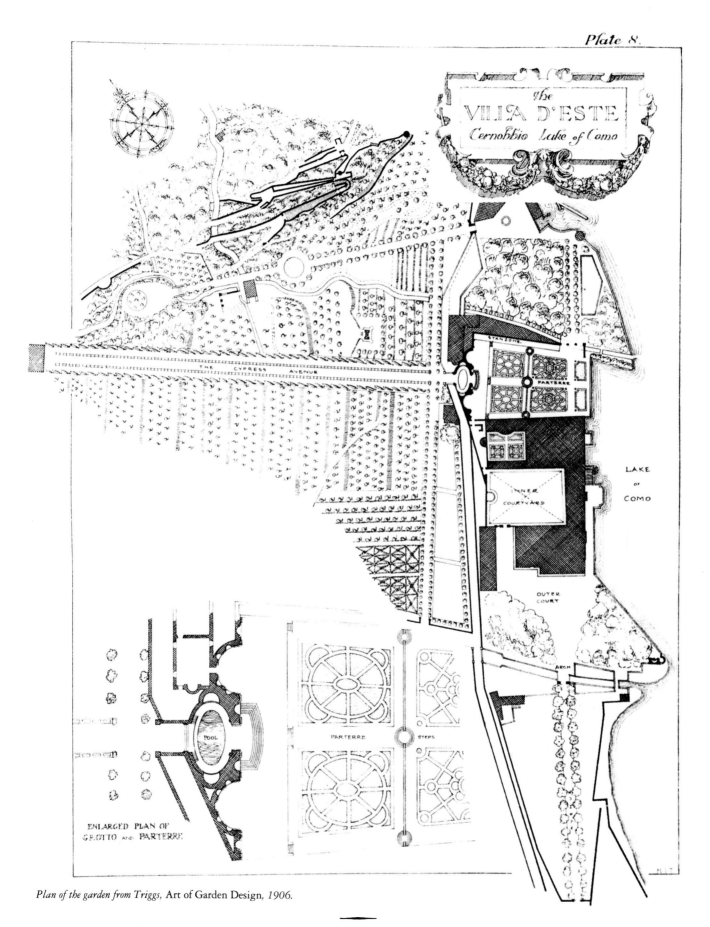

Plate 8.

The
VILLA D'ESTE
Cernobbio Lake of Como

THE CYPRESS AVENUE

STANZONE

PARTERRE

INNER
COURTYARD

LAKE
OF
COMO

OUTER
COURT

ARCH

POOL

PARTERRE

STEPS

ENLARGED PLAN OF
GROTTO AND PARTERRE

Plan of the garden from Triggs, Art of Garden Design, *1906.*

ABOVE: *The mock fortifications above Villa d'Este.*
RIGHT: *The glassed-in dining room overlooks the formal garden and lawns.*

women were dressed up as personifications of Italy's cities.

The Czarina of Russia rented the villa in 1868; its gardens buzzed once more with court intrigue. Since 1873, the Villa d'Este has functioned as a grand hotel, famed world-wide for its elegance.

Villa il Pizzo
Cernobbio

LEFT: *The private port of Villa il Pizzo. The owner is reviving wooden sailboat racing on Lake Como.* ABOVE: *A portion of the long waterfront property showing the main residences.*

*B*ETWEEN HOTEL VILLA D'ESTE and Moltrasio, on a point called Il Pizzo, a retaining garden wall extends about two-thirds of a mile along the waterfront. From the lake, the gardens appear mysterious; a bit is visible, a tantalizing taste, but more of the garden is located away from the immediate shore. Villa il Pizzo's garden is a very private world, with more than half a mile of shady, winding paths, open, high meadows bordered by beeches and oaks, terraces planted with roses and hibiscus, groves of bamboo, and broad, open, formal garden spaces by the lake in the seventeenth-century style.

Originally, the site was an agricultural holding, producing oil and wine in the fifteenth century. Grottoes once used to store the produce still riddle the hillside. The villa was built before 1545 by G. B. Speciano, a senator from Cremona and a papal legate who was involved in the siege of "Il Medeghino," Gian Giacomo de'Medici's castle at Musso. It was inherited by Count Giovanni Mugiasca, who laid out the park, and who in turn left it to the Ospedale Maggiore of Como in 1830. The vice regent of Milan, Archduke Ranieri, summered here. Ranieri planted the two splendid specimens of *Pinus austriaca nigra*. In 1848, the owner Baron Gaetano Ippolito

ABOVE: *A greenhouse tucked against a hillside.*
RIGHT: *Terraces above the formal garden staircase.*

Ciani lost the villa when it was sequestrated because of his political activities. A French woman, Elise Musard, owned it until 1873, when she sold it to Fortunato Volpi Bassani.

The landscaped English park is based largely on Musard's specifications, designed between 1865 and 1871 by the architect Villoresi, who also did the Villa Reale at Monza. The massive octagonal granite mausoleum of the Volpi Bassani family, by architect Luca Beltrami, occupies the choicest site in the garden, a lofty belvedere with splendid views of the lake. This garden has a great variety of features: paths wind past a terraced boat house—built by the Volpi Bassani—and up to an *orrido*, a cliffside cascade with a craggy bridge. Here ferns, camellias, and azaleas are planted with pyramidal white hydrangeas and tall pink begonias. The two formal rectangular gardens lie below the villas on the waterfront level. (There are actually two villas, but one has been boarded up since early in this century when the wife of the owner died in an epidemic. The death chamber is buried deep in the dust of almost a century. By the terms of the last owner's will, this villa was to

be left untouched.) One of these had high bay hedges with low box-edged lawns; the other has a monumental staircase leading to an upper terrace. Both have Baroque fountains. *Olea fragrans* perfumes the house. An upper path leads to a hornbeam pergola and a greenhouse.

When the last of the Volpi Bassani died, the villa passed to a cousin, Raimonda Sanna. She and her husband Gian Paolo Lodigiani use Villa il Pizzo as a base for their sailboat-building and racing business.

Begonias and hibiscus blooming in front of the staircase.

Villa Passalacqua
Moltrasio

LEFT: *Purple irises grow beside a wisteria-covered* tempietto.
ABOVE: *At the bottom of the garden is the frog pool set against a rock garden.*

THE MAIN ROAD to Como dips down at Moltrasio in a detour. Facing Torno on the opposite shore is Villa Passalacqua—a massive, eighteenth-century apricot-colored villa with heavy wrought-iron doors and a balcony teeming with putti. On the villa's terrace level are lawns and a broad staircase that introduces the elliptical carriage drive. The plan of the garden is determined by this drive, dividing the steep hillside into five sections before coming to rest at the gates facing the lakeside road. The garden is constructed on artificial elevations built on enormous stone vaults. Now in a semi-neglected state, the garden retains pleasurable bits and pieces, such as a wisteria-covered *tempietto* next to a large clump of dark purple iris, or an ancient stone wellhead with delicate ironwork. Lower down is a pair of rustic wooden rail fences laden with wisteria. The unexpected appearance of two large, turquoise ceramic Chinese Foo dogs flanking the drive, reveal the tastes of current owner, Elizabeth Kiss Maerth, a scholar of Oriental philosophy.

There are numerous small pools and fountains; twin fishponds with gleaming, bronzy brown statues are found on the upper terrace, and smaller fountains appear here and there. A stepped water channel bordered by thick

ABOVE: *The elaborate wrought-iron doors of Villa Passalacqua.*
RIGHT: *Old pony carts on the lawn in front of the villa.*

bergenias is centered on the slope. By the bottom gate is a lily pool with a whispering fountain of small pagan figures. Behind it is a rock garden with tiny yellow and white blossoms and a vagrant pink tulip. Vocal bullfrogs compete with the barking of guard dogs. Near the bottom of the slope is a large *cinquefoil* parterre design picked out in pebbles.

The counts Lucini-Passalacqua hosted Vincenzo Bellini here between 1829 and 1833. In this villa he conceived his operas *Norma* and *La Sonnambula*. Elizabeth Maerth restored the property in the 1970s. The villa is used for seasonal antiques shows. Its mock medieval entrance gate is adjacent to an exquisite Romanesque church, Sant'-Agata, dating from the eleventh century.

Villa Balbiano

Ossuccio

ALONG THE ROAD FROM Lenno to Ossuccio, a narrow green garden tantalizingly appears for a moment behind high, wrought-iron gates. A lily pool is set behind the gates, within an oval walled enclosure, which opens to disclose the sweep of grassy lawn that descends to the villa beyond. If the front door of the sixteenth-century villa is open, the vista continues through to the water's edge.

The spacing and scale of the villa and its garden are akin to chamber music—intimate, measured, balanced. The former gardener from nearby Balbianello meticulously presides over this garden, which is ablaze with color.

On a spring day the side lawns are covered with tiny marguerites and fallen pink blossoms from the Judas tree. The balustrade of the seawall is laden with blooming white wisteria. Japanese irises stand high above the lily pads, under which goldfish dart. By the edge of the villa are lushly filled flowerbeds and roses climbing up loggia columns.

The villa's name is borrowed from the locality of Balbiano, so-called after the medieval Counts Balbiano. During the fourteenth and fifteenth centuries, the Giovio

ABOVE: *White wisteria clings to the waterside wall.*
RIGHT: *A sheltered side garden.*

FOLLOWING: *Tiny marguerites carpet the lawn in spring.*

family had a noble villa here, which has since been destroyed. Around it were plantations of mulberries for the cultivation of silkworms, and olive trees. Cardinal Tolomeo Gallio, the Giovio's protegé, purchased the property from them in 1596. A new villa was built, probably using the Giovio family's architect, Pellegrino Tibaldi.

Giovanni Battista Giovio bought the property back from Gallio's heirs in 1778. At this time, the gardens were laid out, but the property remained for only nine years in the Giovio family.

The Papal Nuncio at Warsaw, Cardinal Angelo Maria Durini, acquired it in 1787, along with the nearby promontory of Balbianello. A man of epicurean and literary tastes, he amplified and embellished the villa to create a fitting setting for his entertainments. In 1796, the idyll

collapsed with the approach of the Austrian troops; Durini strapped heavy pieces of gold to his body in preparation for an escape across the mountains to Switzerland, and died of a ruptured hernia. His heirs neglected the villa, which was sold in 1872 to the industrialist Gessner family. They transformed the ballroom into a silk factory. In 1930, the villa was scaled down, its side wings demolished and agricultural terrain sold off. The renaissance of the villa and its gardens was due to its next owner, Hermann Hartlaub, who entrusted its restoration to an engineer in 1962. He modified the lakeside approach, whose steps had slid under the waters; he also created the water channel that we see today in the gardens. Villa Balbiano is now owned by Michele Canepa.

Villa Balbianello
Lenno

*V*ILLA BALBIANELLO is more than a garden, it is a spellbinding promontory, weaving its magic on all who approach it. Part of its beauty is that it must be reached by boat. A small launch departs three days a week from the tiny fishing village of Ossuccio, arriving at the villa's southern landing pier, with its wrought-iron gates and pink geraniums. Paths wind up to a terrace, where an ancient Franciscan church stands next to the most captivating port on Lake Como. Walls with a statue of San Carlo Borromeo blessing the waters curve around the miniature harbor, from which a flight of stairs enticingly leads the visitor up into the garden.

Early in the thirteenth century, Franciscans settled the tip of the promontory, building a monastery there. It was still functional in the sixteenth century under Capuchin friars. In 1787, Cardinal Angelo Maria Durini acquired the property, with the intention of using it as an adjunct for entertaining. His main residence was Villa Balbiano at Ossuccio. Coffee was first served in Lombardy at the graceful loggia that overlooks both sides of the promontory. Flanked by two chambers, it was used for recitals and literary discussions in Cardinal Durini's time. Cardinal Durini's heirs sold it to Count Luigi Porri

PRECEDING: *A linden avenue leads down to the ferryboat landing.*
LEFT: *The loggia containing Count Monzino's library.*
ABOVE: *Villa Balbianello seen from Lake Como.*

Lambertenghi, who opposed the Austrian domination of northern Italy and used it to shelter revolutionaries, including the writer and patriot Silvio Pellico, who tutored Lambertenghi's sons. Porri Lambertenghi, in turn, left it to the Marquises Arconati Visconti early in the nineteenth century.

The Arconati Visconti family enlarged the villa and shaped the gardens. The delightful balustrades are carved with their family crest—an infant being swallowed by a serpent—alternating with seesawing putti. The Marchioness Arconati Visconti's lover was killed shielding her from an assassin's bullet. Grieving, she shut the villa for thirty years, until 1911.

At this point, the Bostonian General Butler Ames picnicked on the grounds and fell in love with Balbianello. For eight years, he persistently attempted to purchase the property. It was bought unexpectedly by the German kaiser's younger son, Prince Eitel Friedrich, on the eve of the First World War, and then confiscated by the Italian government. General Ames was able to acquire it after the

war, in 1919. With the assistance of his friend, Major-General Cecil Albert Heydeman, Ames restored the gardens. General Ames died in 1954, leaving the property to his nieces and nephews. In 1974, Balbianello was sold to Count Guido Monzino, who modified the gardens, eliminating the flowerbeds to create lawns. He replaced statues of saints with secular ones. The villa and grounds remain as Count Monzino left them, willed to the Fondo Ambiente Italiano. Monzino's library and a museum devoted to his polar and mountain explorations keep his personality alive here. He loved this property and chose to be buried in the garden when he died in 1988.

Balbianello occupies the promontory Il Dosso d'Avedo, also called Lavedo, separating the bays of Venus and Diana. Clipped laurel covers the southern slope, which features an allée of pollarded linden trees. Cypresses are planted strategically for dramatic accents. In spring, the masses of pink azaleas against varied shades of green are an unforgettable sight.

ABOVE: *The balcony is carved with seesawing putti and the Visconti family emblem.*
RIGHT: *The most poetic port of Lake Como; statues of religious figures bless the waters, a reminder of the villa's monastic past.*

Villa Vigoni

Loveno

LEFT: *Spring irises beyond the villa.*
ABOVE: *Giosuè Argenti's statue of Luigia Vigoni and her children.*

$\mathcal{V}$ILLA VIGONI, formerly Villa Mylius, was left to the government of Germany by an Italian citizen, Don Ignazio Vigoni, at his death in 1983, to be used as a center for cultural, political, and scientific exchange between Italy and Germany. This goal continues the tradition of hospitality established here by Heinrich Mylius in the nineteenth century to men of the arts from both countries. Among his friends, Mylius counted the writers Johann Wolfgang von Goethe and Alessandro Manzoni, the naturalist and explorer Eduard Rüppel, and the numismatist from the Brera Museum, Gaetano Cattaneo. The villa descended through the widow of Heinrich's only son, Giulio. Luigia Mylius was remarried to an employee of her father-in-law's, Ignazio Vigoni. Their son married a descendant of Heinrich's brother, Cattula Mylius, who lived to the advanced age of ninety-seven, with her unmarried son, the second Ignazio Vigoni.

The park comprises about twenty acres of the total property, which consists of one hundred acres of agricultural fields and wooded slopes, as well as four villas and assorted outbuildings.

On the western shore of Lake Como, a road winds slowly up to Loveno from the town of Menaggio. A coun-

ABOVE AND RIGHT: *Views of the park of Villa Vigoni where outdoor concerts are performed.*

Statue of an angel by Giosuè Argenti.

try lane separates the main villa from an administration building. The site is splendid: from the hillside the view encompasses the peninsula of Bellagio, both arms of the lake, and the eastern mountains. In the foreground is the tower of the parish church, San Domenico, whose bells peal out over the hush of the gardens.

Nestled on the carefully sculpted slopes, the villa is surrounded by superb specimen trees and exotic shrubs. Paths snake through the lawns in the English landscape style, around a small pool, up to the small neoclassical memorial chapel dedicated to Giulio Mylius, and around strategically placed statues. Landscape architect Luigi Balzaretto reorganized the terraced vineyards around 1840. He planted specimen trees, often alongside faster growing trees, in order to provide temporary visual pleasure until the specimen trees had grown to a substantial size. An enormous *Cypressus funebris,* brought by Rüppel from the Himalayas, unfortunately had to be removed after storm damage; however, among the remaining trees are sizeable examples of *Pinus pinea, Juniperus sabina,* and sequoia. A statue of Luigia Vigoni, widowed after only one month of marriage to Giulio Mylius, shows her surrounded by her children from her second marriage. This statue, as well as one of an angel rising in flight, was carved by Giosuè Argenti. The beauty of this garden-park derives from the massing of trees and the contrasting shades of their foliage. The garden reflects the enthusiasm of the nineteenth-century lake residents for the naturalistic romantic landscape garden, and the rage for collecting exotic specimens. It is a fitting setting for Don Ignazio's birthday anniversary concerts which are held every August.

Villa Bagatti Valsecchi

Cardano di Grandola

A SINGULAR CLIFFSIDE GARDEN exists at twelve hundred feet between Lakes Como and Lugano. This is a garden belonging more to the mountains embracing Lake Como than to its waters, yet Lake Como and its Isola Comacina are visible from the highest ridge of the garden. The little village of Cardano di Grandola is found off the road leading from Menaggio to Porlezza. A group of stone houses etched with *graffito* designs sets off the forecourt of the Villa Bagatti Valsecchi. Between the stone paving grow flowers, including calendula. One wall is frescoed with Saints Roch and Anthony Abbot, both protectors against the plague. Geraniums spill out over the loggia balcony.

Partially built in 1700 by the Guaita family, the property was passed by inheritance from the Barons Galbiati in 1896 to the Bagatti Valsecchi, who raised the villa by a story and by 1911 added the eastern loggia and towers.

The garden is divided into two portions, the "old" garden dating from the 1930s bordering the house along the ravine, and the "new" garden of open terraced lawns and flowerbeds to the west, created in the 1940s and 1950s. The layout of both gardens was designed by a past

ABOVE: *The lawn of the "new" garden below the swimming pool.*
RIGHT: *A corner under ancient cypresses.*

president of the Lombardy Horticultural Society, Baron Pasino Bagatti Valsecchi, father of the current owner. The old garden, with its little pond and collection of conifers, ferns, maples, rhododendrons, and rock gardens, runs east from the house. This section looks across the gorge to the mountains of Legnone, Grona, and Grigna. The opposite slope, planted with pines, firs, and larches, is part of the property. Hundreds of feet below, the river Sanagra flows, its roaring waterfalls clearly audible in the gardens high above. *Pyracantha, berberis, erica, buddleia, Chamaecyparis obtusa nana,* and *Pinus mugo* grow on the steep cliffs, and are tended by courageous gardeners suspended on cables. The highest and lowest points of the gardens vary by four hundred feet.

The new garden reveals the keen interest in flowers of the present owners, architect Pier Fausto Bagatti Valsecchi and his wife. Passing through a door in the loggia, one

steps down to the lowest terrace level. The terraces, rearranged as open lawns, were originally cultivated with olives; now cypresses and hedges define the levels. The retaining walls shelter flowerbeds and also provide rock-garden sites. A rustic wooden fence runs along the steps bordering the cliff's face. Perennials—irises, roses, columbines, alpine plants, *buddleia,* lupins, phlox, and fuchsias—make up the spring borders. An extensive collection of dahlias and potted Korean chrysanthemums bloom in the late summer and early fall. A swimming pool is a recent addition. This garden is a labor of love; Baron Bagatti Valsecchi is deeply interested in the history and preservation of Italy's historic villas and gardens and serves on the board of the Fondo per l'Ambiente Italiano.

This most romantic of garden sites makes use of the vast, dramatic surroundings, and careful placement of trees for their shapes and tones of foliage.

Villa la Collina
Griante

AMONG THE DISTINGUISHED summer residents of Lake Como, the first chancellor of the Federal Republic of Germany, Konrad Adenauer, has left a lasting memorial of his annual visits. His villa, La Collina, is now an international meeting place, the Fondazione Konrad Adenauer, established in 1977.

Adenauer was fortunate to find this site at the village of Griante, above the traffic of Cadenabbia, with views toward the promontory of Bellagio. The villa was built in 1890, and caps the *collina*, or hill. Adenauer first rented the villa from a French family. In 1977, the foundation purchased the property. It became Adenauer's "small chancery." Here the chancellor sat for his portraits by Graham Sutherland and Oskar Kokoschka. It was a meeting place for politicians, scientists, economists, and men of letters. Under the long, rose-covered pergolas that mark the hillside terraces, Adenauer took walks, chatting with his guests or drafting his memoirs.

The beautiful park is filled with enormous pines and red beeches. Camellias, azaleas, and roses contrast with the ornamental palms and magnolias. The loggias of the buff-colored villa look out on garden terraces below, with Bellagio and the mountains facing the villa across the lake.

ABOVE: *The horizon of the small swimming pool merges with that of the lake.*
RIGHT: *Olive oil jars used as planters along the path by the villa.*

Villa Carlotta
Tremezzo

LEFT: *The gates of Villa Carlotta frame a pool surrounded by tall hedges of* Laurocerasi.
ABOVE AND FOLLOWING: *The rock gardens of Carlotta.*

SPRING ON LAKE COMO is linked firmly in the minds of many Italians with Villa Carlotta. When the rhododendrons and azaleas are massed on the hillsides of Tremezzo, it is an incredible spectacle.

The gardens were laid out in two phases—the formal Italian terraced gardens, which rise from street level to the villa, and the English landscape garden extending along the lake to the north of the villa. One enters the formal portion passing through high hedges to a charming fountain of a putto and dolphin in front of a lacy, wrought-iron gate, which once led to the boat landing. This landing was the subject of Henry Wadsworth Longfellow's poem, "By Sommariva's Garden Gate," which muses on the perfect beauty of the site as the poet sat on the marble steps listening to the water. In front of the villa, double staircases lead to narrow terraces right and left. On one there is a heavily laden orange arbor. Roses and vines creep along the surface of the retaining walls, and goldfish and turtles swim in the low basins at the stair landing.

The landscape garden is approached by first passing through a dark jungle glade filled with ferns. Out in the sunlight, the paths wind across lanes, through hedges of

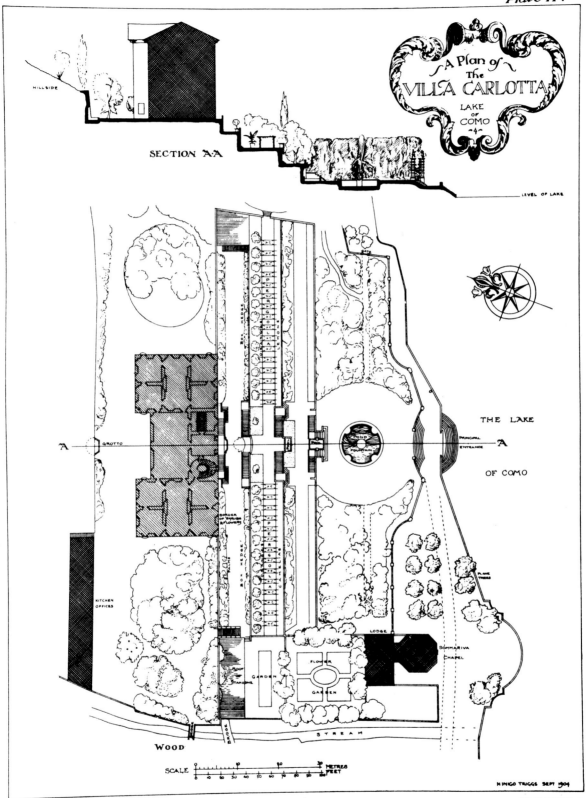

Plate 11.

SECTION AA

HILLSIDE

LEVEL OF LAKE

A Plan of
The
VILLA CARLOTTA
LAKE
OF
COMO

THE LAKE

OF COMO

GROTTO

A   A

PRINCIPAL
ENTRANCE

POND
FOUNTAIN

KITCHEN
OFFICES

BORDER
OF SHRUBS
& FLOWERS

BOX HEDGE

BOX HEDGE

LODGE

BOMMARIVA
CHAPEL

ROOF
OF
STANDING

GARDEN

FLOWER

GARDEN

WOOD

STREAM

SCALE   METRES
FEET

INIGO TRIGGS SEPT 1904

West, Neomen photo lith

LEFT: *Villa Carlotta is known for its paths lined with azaleas and rhododendrons.*
ABOVE: *Villa Carlotta, from Triggs,* Art of Garden Design, *1906.*

rhododendrons, to a belvedere and then back across an open lawn planted with a variety of conifers, palms, and exotics. Rock gardens cover the upper hillside. At intervals there are views of the lake, adding to the beauty of the place.

Since the early nineteenth century, when the villa was owned by Count Sommariva, it has enjoyed a reputation for hospitality and an accessible art collection. Stendhal featured it as the "Casa Sommariva" in *La Chartreuse de Parme*. Today it functions as a private museum, showing works of Bertel Thorvaldsen, Antonio Canova, and Francesco Hayez. Among the paintings are nineteenth-century views of the antique lake boats and the villa *en fête* with fireworks.

The villa itself was built as a summer residence for the Marquis Antonio Giorgio Clerici between 1690 and 1743. President of the Lombard Senate and a Milanese banker, he passed the villa on to his descendant Claudia Clerici, who in 1795 married Giovanni Battista Sommariva di Lodi. Sommariva rose politically to become the leader of the Second Cisalpine Republic. Across the lake at Bellagio, his political opponent Francesco Melzi, vice president of the Napoleonic Italian Republic, was creating the lavish Villa Melzi. Not to be outdone, Sommariva embellished the facade of his villa, adding the clock and roof balustrades and extending the park.

In 1840, his widowed daughter-in-law sold the villa but retained the former Clerici chapel as the Sommariva mausoleum. A few years later, the Villa Sommariva became the property of Princess Marianna of Nassau, wife of Albrecht of Prussia. Their daughter Carlotta received the villa as a wedding gift when she married Prince George, duke of Saxe-Meiningen. Carlotta's name has been identified with the villa since that time. She entertained lavishly; her green and white liveried barge was a familiar sight on Lake Como. It is her landscape garden that is now admired—planted with sequoias, banana trees, palms, one hundred and fifty varieties of rhododendron, Japanese *cryptomeria*, tropical orchids—all exotics in vogue with the gardeners of her era. Villa Carlotta was confiscated by the Italian government as alien property during the First World War. Now a corporation maintains it, permitting public access.

Tropical vegetation at the villa.

Villa la Quiete
Bolvedro

VILLA LA QUIETE, also known as Villa Sola Cabiati, stands proudly by the roadside between Bolvedro and Tremezzo. Most waterfront properties on this side of Lake Como are separated from their landing piers by the road built in the early nineteenth century. These villas were in the past approached by mule paths across the back hills, or more frequently by water. La Quiete's landing steps descend in graceful curves and the impulse is irresistible to run down to the water's edge, where a pair of traditional *lucia* boats are moored.

The garden is directly across the road behind elaborate gates. Its uniqueness lies in the pebble-patterned arabesque parterre designs, interspersed in early spring with beds of pansies, later replaced by begonias. Pink roses twine up the lamp posts. This eighteenth-century formal garden has been maintained intact—an exception to the general trend on the lakes to revamp gardens in English landscape style.

The central block of the villa was built in the early eighteenth century for the Duchess del Carretto from Piedmont. It subsequently passed through the ownership of the Brentano family to Duke Gian Galeazzo Serbelloni. His principal residence was the Villa Serbelloni, across the lake at Bellagio. Villa la Quiete was used as a *dépendance* for overflow houseguests, and for nine summers housed his son and his son's tutor, the poet Giuseppe Parini. Abate Parini is said to have composed here part of his poem "Il Mattino," in which he sets forth the proper conduct for a gentleman. The villa passed through the female lines by marriage to the Busca and Sola families. It is now owned by Contessa Sola Cabiati.

The name "La Quiete" referred to its peaceful location on the Gulf of San Lorenzo.

ABOVE: *The steps in front of the villa descend to the lake.*
RIGHT: *Pebbled arabesques.*

Villa Melzi
Bellagio

VILLA MELZI is a monument to neoclassicism. In the villa, its chapel, and the gardens too, there is a cool precision and rationale. Despite the thousands of public visitors annually, the grounds are meticulously maintained by its owner, Count Ludovic Gallarati-Scotti. His ancestor, Francesco Melzi d'Eril, duke of Lodi, a personal friend of Napoleon, helped shape Italian independence and unification. It was Francesco who built the villa between 1808 and 1810, and planted the first trees, a cedar of Lebanon and a giant poplar, which survive to this day. He commissioned the sculptor Giovanni Battista Comolli to design the tombs in the little chapel at the far tip of the garden. Comolli also made the large sculpture of Beatrice and Dante, which stands near a Moorish kiosk by the water's edge, and is said to have inspired Franz Liszt to compose the Dante Sonata. More likely, it was his mistress Countess d'Agoult's reading of the *Divine Comedy* in the romantic kiosk, while they were guests here, which led to the composition.

The guest list was long and illustrious: Stendhal, Metternich, Austrian emperors Ferdinand and Francis Joseph I, Viceroy Eugène de Beauharnais, and Empress Maria Fedorovna. Two wonderful Montezuma pines stand

ABOVE: *A cypress, Montezuma pine, and begonias.*
RIGHT: *Azaleas and rhododendrons cover the hillsides of Villa Melzi; a pollarded alleé borders the lake.*

along the shore—enormous specimens; these are believed to have been among the saplings dispatched from Mexico by the ill-fated Emperor Maximilian.

Of the original garden, the portion in front of the villa remains intact, with its statues of Apollo and Meleager by Michelangelo's pupil, Guglielmo della Porta. The cool, measured tone of the semicircular waterfront terrace is enhanced by the pollarded allée of plane trees that frame the villa along the shore. A change of mood is found in the small Japanese garden with its pond near the entrance, and the grotto with Etruscan artifacts within. The actual size of the garden is not vast, yet it contains great variety, with vistas beyond the garden of water, olive groves, and far-off snowcapped mountains. The chief beauty of the garden is its display in May of azaleas, camellias, and rhododendrons, cascading color across sloping lawns. In any season the exceptional collection of well-labeled trees is worth a visit.

Villa Trotti
San Giovanni

BEYOND VILLA MELZI and Villa Trivulzio, the neighboring villa is Villa Trotti. In a chain of stately villas, each with important landscape gardens, Villa Trotti and Villa Trivulzio are actually connected by a small iron bridge spanning a torrent, a reminder that they were once both owned by Count Gerli.

Now split up into condominiums, the villa is one of the oldest in this zone. It was rebuilt in the eighteenth century and then redone in 1850 in Moorish style. It faces west; the waterfront railings to its landing stage are covered with wisteria. Credit for laying out the landscape park is due to the Marquis Lodovico Trotti-Bentivoglio, whose wife was lady-in-waiting to Queen Margherita of Italy. Many distinguished guests strolled through the gardens and the allée of splendid plane trees backed by high hedges of hornbeam. Among these guests were novelist Alessandro Manzoni, poet Giuseppe Giusti, Prince Maximilian, and Francis I of Austria.

To the north side of the villa stretches a vast lawn planted with a huge magnolia, a massive red rhododendron, an *Acer negundo*, a cluster of stone pines, and *Fagus sylvatica*. A rare *Quercus stenophilla* and some spectacular specimens of *Cedrus atlantica* are of special importance

ABOVE: *The landing steps of Villa Trotti.*
RIGHT: *The parks of Villa Trotti and Villa San Giovanni were once linked by this bridge.*

here. Groves of dense bamboo grow by the entrance gates, and more bamboo and *Trachycarpus fortunei* are by the waterside. The garden was also noted for its tropical vegetation and for a Japanese summerhouse on a little island surrounded by aquatic plants. Enormous fuchsias once lined the paths.

Villa Trotti's park is a haven of quiet beauty in the spring, when its wisteria, azaleas, and rhododendrons bloom.

Grand Hotel Villa Serbelloni
Bellagio

LEFT: *Late spring azaleas.*
ABOVE: *The garden terrace staircase.*

*T*HE GRAND HOTEL VILLA SERBELLONI occupies the northern end of town like a dowager, supremely self-confident, with the elegance of a past era. The hotel was originally built as a villa for a Milanese family, the Frizzani. By 1854, the central block was built to the plans of architect Vantini. Later, side wings were added to create a luxurious hotel, catering to a royal clientele. Around 1870, the Grand Hotel Bellagio was opened. Eventually, at the time of the Second World War, the name was changed to Grand Hotel Villa Serbelloni, after the Villa Serbelloni higher up on the promontory.

The gardens retain the *darsena*, or boathouse, and the lower formal parterre terrace from the period of the Frizzani family. About twenty years ago the terrace lost a portion of its parterre to make room for a swimming pool. Balustraded twin staircases rise from the beach to the parterre level, and wind up to the upper terrace on which the hotel is set. The gardens have been abbreviated over the years by the construction of outbuildings. A palm walk, which leads past azalea-covered slopes, terminates at the waterfront. It ends at the site of a former Roman bath marked by a small pavilion. This bath was once filled by the periodic flooding of the lake. Over the years,

the flooding ceased, so the waters became stagnant and the bath was eventually filled in. The lakeside terraces have a splendid view of the Tremezzina—a group of towns lining the shores opposite Bellagio. The terraces are open to the sun, and the gardens spill over with flowering vines and roses throughout the summer months.

RIGHT AND PRECEDING: *The parterre terrace below the hotel and its splendid views of Tremezzina.*

Villa Serbelloni
now Fondazione Rockefeller
Bellagio

VILLA SERBELLONI, now the seat of the Fondazione Rockefeller, has a long, romantic, and infinitely varied history. Besides being the largest park on Lake Como, it has the distinction of having introduced a number of plants to the lake.

The point of Bellagio is traditionally recognized as the site of La Tragoedia, the villa built by Pliny the Younger in A.D. 63. The tip of the promontory rises high above the lake, separating the two arms, Como and Lecco. The name given to the villa, La Tragoedia, alludes to the custom of Roman tragic actors wearing heeled shoes, to give them added height on the stage.

Eight hundred granite steps were built from the shore to the summit, from which, according to legend, Countess Borgomanero pushed her discarded lovers in the middle ages. At that time there was a pirate's stronghold on the hillside. On the order of Galeazzo II, head of the powerful Visconti family, the castle was destroyed.

A description of the property in 1499, when it belonged to the Marchesino Stanga, mentions a garden, probably of a strictly utilitarian nature. Stanga planted trees on what had formerly been a barren hilltop. Today it is covered with a forest of chestnut, pine, and beech trees. Sloping down to the town of Bellagio are vineyards and

olive groves. Olives and other fruit trees, including figs, citrus, and oranges existed there by 1558. The Sfondrati family inherited the property from the Stangas, and built the present villa in 1605. A visitor, Filippo Meda, wrote in 1636 of the *Olea fragrans* and autumn perfumes of the juniper, larch, oak, chestnut, olives, and sunbathed stone walls hidden by pear trees with all kinds of quinces and pomegranates. Garden paths traced in ordered decay were flanked by roses and fruit trees, and tasty capers. The villa was transformed by Duke Alessandro Serbelloni, who inherited it from the last of the Sfondrati in 1788. A collector of rare specimen plants, he is responsible for the form of the gardens as we see them today; the formal terraces below the villa date from his time.

By 1875, Villa Serbelloni had the first magnolias, mimosa, pink oleander, cedars, and palms on Lake Como. Between 1868 and 1885, the villa was leased to the Hotel Grande Bretagne as an annex for overflow guests. In a similar vein, it served as an annex for the Grand Hotel Bellagio from 1905 until 1930. Gabriel Fauré, who stayed there in September of 1908, wrote his "L'amour sous les lauriers-roses" on the terrace shaded by an oak which is now seven or eight hundred years old and still thriving. Fauré described strolling along paths in the afternoon with trailing plants, camellias, magnolias, myrtles, "pomegranates with trunks gnarled like plaited ropes," oranges, lemons, "steely blue cacti erect as swords, huge fleshy-leaved aloes....The oleanders sag beneath the weight of their clusters....The overheated earth and the clumps of flowers give out clouds of odors and perfumes such as one inhales on any warm morning in the humid atmosphere of the Mercato Nuovo at Florence. And above all these exhalations the *Olea fragrans* sheds its powerful aroma: no flowering tree emits a subtler, more pervasive odor than this far-eastern olive that has been acclimatized on these shores" (Millard, *The Italian Lakes*, 1958).

An American heiress, Princess della Torre e Tasso, née Ella Walker, purchased Villa Serbelloni in 1930. In 1959 she gave it to the Fondazione Rockefeller to be used as an international conference and study center. The foundation has removed a number of storm-damaged trees and permits the public to tour the gardens. The great attractions of the property are its site, the splendid views in all directions, and the variety of trees in its vast park.

Villa il Monastero

Varenna

THE SITE OF VILLA IL MONASTERO, as that of Villa i Cipressi, was settled by refugees forced from Isola Comacina when Holy Roman Emperor Frederick Barbarossa's troops ravaged their island. Cistercian nuns of Saint Mary Magdalene built their monastery here in 1208. Entrusted with a mission to recruit penitent fallen women, the nuns, in turn, became so lax in their behavior that San Carlo Borromeo intervened with Pope Pius V in 1569 to close the monastery.

Shortly afterwards, it was bought by Paolo Mornico, whose son Lelio spent vast sums on its transformation. Between 1609 and 1619 Lelio Mornico created the garden, extending the lakefront area with landfill. Mornico's delightful garden was lauded by Sigismondo Boldoni in *Larius*, published in 1617. The property became known as Villa Laelia for its owner.

In his poem "Il Monastero, loco ameno del Signor Lelio Mornico," the seventeenth-century poet Luigi Rusca wondered whether he should describe the villa as a dwelling for mortals or for gods.

In 1899, a German, Walter Kess, became the owner and restored the house and garden; in 1904, he bought additional property to create a long promenade toward

LEFT: *The boathouse and terraced gardens of Il Monastero.*
ABOVE: *The garden is liberally adorned with statuary.*

Fiumelatte, ending in a kiosk. The writer Antonio Fogazzaro, often a guest here, used it as the setting for his comedy, *Nadejde*. At the time of the First World War, Villa il Monastero was confiscated by the Italian government. It subsequently became the property of Marco de Marchi, who left it to the state to be used as a center of scientific studies. Enrico Fermi taught physics here, as recalled by an updated Latin inscription mentioning *atoma volventia*, or atom bomb. The villa continues to function as a conference site together with the adjacent Villa i Cipressi.

The villa is squeezed up against a steep slope, with a lengthy terrace along the shore. Bits and pieces of antique architectural fragments appear in every nook and cranny—old wellheads, twisted columns to frame views, and inscriptions. A monumental, precipitous staircase, leading to a little neoclassical temple, has balustrades copied from Villa Balbianello. Along an upper path is a sculpture group, The Clemency of Titus, unfinished at the death of its sculptor, Giovanni Battista Comolli, in 1830. This sculpture originally came from the Villa Bagatti Valsecchi at Cardano.

In May, the wisteria winds along the waterside. Pale pink roses contrast with the red of the Japanese maples and dark cypresses. Palms, camphor, various citrus fruits, and oleander are found in the garden, but the three-hundred-year-old magnolia is its pride.

Villa i Cipressi
Varenna

LEFT: *Water lilies, roses, peonies, acanthus, and magnolias planted by the water's edge.*
ABOVE: *A putto fountain and goldfish in the courtyard basin.*

AS THE SUN shifts with the seasons on Lake Como, the climate of the town of Varenna changes dramatically. In the summer, one heads for the covered walkways by the port to shelter from the blistering sun. In the winter, the temperature is frigid with icy winds and little sunlight. Despite this, two gardens of adjacent villas thrive and share one of the loveliest vistas of the lake. Varenna is opposite the Punta di Bellagio, whose peninsula cleaves the waters of Lecco and Como. From the terraced waterside paths of Villa il Monastero and Villa i Cipressi, this view can be savored.

Villa i Cipressi's garden consists of a series of descending terraces. There is a progression of shaded and open space, winding pebbled paths, and belvederes. In the spring, the walls and balcony railings are laden with wisteria, whose pale lavender contrasts with the dark massive cypresses along the main flight of steps. The shore curves eastward to Villa il Monastero, with a continuous curtain of cypresses linking the two villas. A sunken garden by i Cipressi's boathouse is filled with roses, hydrangeas, and peonies. Acanthus flourishes under magnolia trees. The villa has a long history dating back to the evacuation of the Isola Comacina with the arrival of the troops of Frederick Barbarossa, the Holy Roman emperor, in 1169. The Serponti family fled Comacina and settled here. Baron Isimbardi, the director of the Milan mint, bought the property at the beginning of the nineteenth century. It functioned as a hotel under the Venini family, hosting the Austrian Emperor Ferdinand in 1838. Before the First World War, it became the property of Sir Richard Sutton, passing through his family until the late 1930s when it was bought by the publisher Accame. Since 1980, it has been owned by the city of Varenna and functions as a scientific and cultural institution, the Villa i 'Cipressi Association, in conjunction with the neighboring Villa il Monastero.

Three sides of the villa form a courtyard, on one wall of which are found the following lines from a Christopher Marlowe poem: "Running waters to whose falls melodious birds sing madrigals." Framing the view of the lake is a vine-covered pergola, well-loved by the lake's birds, as is the trickling fountain in the center of the courtyard.

ABOVE: *Ivy covering the courtyard loggia.*
RIGHT: *Wisteria and agave border the hillside paths.*
FOLLOWING: *A monkey puzzle tree, cypress, and magnolias along the shore. Villa il Monastero is in the distance.*

LAKE MAGGIORE

*L*ACUS VERBANUS was the Roman name for Lake Maggiore, probably in reference to its green, wooded shores. This was actually a more fitting name than Maggiore, for *maggiore*, literally translated, means "the greatest," and it is not, in fact, the largest lake in Italy.

Lake Maggiore is forty miles in length and is the westernmost of the great Italian lakes. Fifteen percent of it falls within the Swiss province of Ticino—on the southwestern shore is the Italian town of Arona, at the northern tip is the Swiss town of Locarno. In Italy, the lake forms the border between Piedmont and Lombardy. Perhaps the name Maggiore derives from the Maggia River, which feeds the lake from the north and flows through it to empty into the Po. Compared to Lakes Como and Garda, Maggiore has a broader, less enclosed character, with the dis-

tant peaks of the Lepontine Alps marking a border to the north.

John Ruskin preferred Lake Maggiore over the other northern lakes. Perhaps he was captivated, as are so many visitors, by the Borromean Isles that punctuate the widest area of the lake. Whether viewed from the shores of Stresa and Baveno, or from the high slopes of Monte Mottarone, the islands add touches of pure fantasy. The ten-tiered, wedding-cake-shaped garden of Isola Bella, anchored at one end by its Baroque palace, is pure enchantment. Isola Pescatori is an opera-set fishing village where the residents gather to skip rope together in the evening on the quay after the tourist boats have departed for the day. The third island, Isola Madre, is covered by a vast garden, less formal and rigid

ABOVE: Lucias *in the port of Isola dei Pescatori.*
RIGHT: *A passageway on Isola Madre.*

than its neighbor Isola Bella. At night the large empty villa stands sentinel over flocks of decorative, exotic birds that inhabit the island.

The lake has seen many power struggles over the centuries. The ruins of the two Castelli di Cannero, off the shores of Cannero, were once linked by a drawbridge. In the fifteenth century, these castles were the headquarters of the five Mazzardi brothers, who terrorized the lake as brigands. Duke Filippo Visconti at last dispatched a retaliatory force of four hundred men to subdue the brothers, who barricaded themselves in the castles for two years. In 1439, Visconti gave Vitaliano Borromeo title to most of the Visconti properties on Lake Maggiore, including the Castelli, which he eventually wrested away from the Mazzardi. The Visconti, subsequently, handed over their fortress at Angera in 1450, giving the Borromeos virtual control of the lake.

During the nineteenth-century movement for Italian independence, the nationalist leader Giuseppe Garibaldi fought at Laveno where the Austrians garrisoned a fortress. Lake Maggiore has the very first of the ubiquitous monuments to Garibaldi, erected at Luino to commemorate his raising a new army there after his defeat at Custoza.

Besides San Carlo Borromeo, who was born at his family castle at Arona, Lake Maggiore claims as native sons the painter Bernardo Luini, born at Luino, and Marshal Luigi Cadorna, commander in chief of Italy's armed forces in the First World War, born at Pallanza.

Lake Maggiore's distinguished guest list of summer residents includes the writer Alessandro Manzoni, who lived at Lesa in the Villa Stampa and also at Cerro del Lago Maggiore. Conductor Arturo Toscanini also often stayed on Isola San Giovanni.

Apart from the Borromean properties, the majority of important villas date from the second half of the nineteenth century, when Queen Margherita and King Umberto I led their court to Stresa for annual visits. Queen Victoria occupied a villa at the next town, Baveno. Other

ABOVE: *Rooftops of Stresa.*

pretty villas were centered around Belgirate, Meina, Ghiffa, Cannero, and Verbania.

The great appeal of Lake Maggiore, beyond its natural beauty, is its climate—portions of it are extremely sheltered in the winter, such as Cannero, known as the Cannero Riviera, which lack the troublesome wind and dust of

ABOVE: *The Borromean Islands.*
FOLLOWING: *Lake Maggiore from Monte Mottarone.*

the French and Italian Rivieras. Because of this mild climate, and its plentiful water supply, the area around Pallanza became noted for its plant nurseries in the second half of the nineteenth century. This was a time of botanical explorations and interest in new exotic plants. Many plants appeared in Italy for the first time on Lake Maggiore, imported by its fashionable summer residents. Lake Maggiore's garden parks are now the beneficiaries of this trend. Trees planted to show off variations of shades and textures are now fully mature and magnificent. Rhododendrons and azaleas were propagated on the lake; Isola Madre and Villa Taranto have exceptional collections of these shrubs.

The gardens of Maggiore were created in the Belle Epoque style, mixing art with nature, carving out artificial grottoes, building rugged, rocky walled paths with seemingly natural gorges, and spanning carefully laid out streams and pools with little bridges. The lack of broad, even spaces in the gardens demanded natural, rather than formal, layouts. Villas are typically set back about 160 feet from the shore, and are raised up about sixty feet above water level. A small terrace serves as a platform-belvedere for the villa from which the lake can be viewed. The garden is usually set off from the main road by a balustrade. Besides the collections of rare trees and plants, the villas often had greenhouses to cultivate orchids and bedding flowers.

Stendhal summed up his feelings about the lake saying, "When you have a heart and a shirt, you must sell your shirt and see the surroundings of Lake Maggiore" (Binda, *Romantico Lago Maggiore*, 1990).

Isola Bella

The southern end of Isola Bella showing the rear of the amphitheater and towers housing the water pumps.

O N A MISTY DAY, Isola Bella rises up from the waters of Lake Maggiore like a mirage. From the shoreline it resembles a ten-tiered wedding cake, or a ship with multiple decks. At one end of the island, the Baroque palace of the Borromeos looms up by an unfinished port. Indeed, the original plan was to re-shape the tiny island (less than a quarter of a mile long) into the form of a ship: the northern end was to be the prow, and a towering spire above the palace was planned to represent the foremast.

To reach the gardens one must pass through the vast rooms of the palace. A room built to look like a grotto, encrusted with seashells and coral, contains a model of the gardens. The tapestry hall opens out into a small, rounded garden courtyard. Diana's Courtyard and the adjacent Theater of Hercules are mere preludes to the terraces above and are angled to lead the visitor up to a central axis, cutting through parterres to the amphitheater. This architectural set-piece is filled with statues in scalloped niches, topped by obelisks and a unicorn. The amphitheater rises four terraces above the parterre area, creating a spectacular belvedere. Behind it, extending to the southern tip of the island, is another formal parterre

133

LEFT AND FOLLOWING: *The small formal parterre behind the amphitheater.*
ABOVE: *Isola Bella from Dal Re's* Ville di delizia, *1726.*

and pumps that supply the garden with water. The hydraulic system was devised by the Roman engineer Mora-Torreggia.

The island took its name from Isabella, wife of Count Carlo Borromeo III. In 1632, he levelled the terrain and began construction with architect Angelo Crivelli. His son, Count Vitaliano IV, finished the gardens by 1671, guided by the architects Carlo Fontana and Francesco Castelli.

Bishop Gilbert Burnet visited the gardens in 1685 and described them in *Some Letters* as "certainly the loveliest spots of ground in the world, there is nothing in all Italy that can be compared to them, they have the full view of the lake, and the ground rises so sweetly in them that nothing can be imagined like the terraces here." In the first quarter of the eighteenth century, the terraces were still sparse in vegetation compared to the lush growth we encounter today. Yet by 1730, Charles de Brosses was impressed by the jasmine, oranges, and pomegranates growing on every level. Now there is a wide variety of plants and flowers, including orchids, rhododendrons, azaleas, oleanders, camellias, *Taxus baccata, Laurus camphora,* cork, bread, tea, and coffee trees. These trees have long since grown out of proportion to the terraces, obscuring the layout of the garden.

Isola Bella's exotic beauty was enjoyed for two days by Napoleon and his entourage in August 1797, after his conquest of Italy at the Battle of Marengo. It is to be wondered what he thought of the Borromeo family motto; *Humilitas,* spelt out in a *broderie* parterre. The perfumes that waft across the terraces and the white peacocks perched on balustrades are unchanged with time.

135

Isola Madre

*L*ESS PUBLICIZED THAN ISOLA BELLA is its sister island, Isola Madre, the largest of the Borromean properties. Unlike the theatrical pomp and fantasy of Isola Bella, Isola Madre enchants by its naturalness. In the spring, it is a blaze of color, complete with exotic birds and foliage-framed views of the surrounding lake. It is an arborist's delight, so varied are its plantings. Unlike the other Borromean islands of Isola dei Pescatori and Isola Bella, this one lacks a resident population. The one restaurant closes, the garden gates pull shut, and the last ferry chugs off to Pallanza at dusk. The villa is occupied by lifeless marionettes and antique dolls; its chapel, by departed members of the Borromeo family. Seen from Isola dei Pescatori in the evening, Isola Madre looms silent and dark in the water.

In the spring, Chinese pheasant chicks wander among fallen camellia blossoms and snow-white peacocks trail their train-like tail feathers on lush lawns. In 1797, Napoleon came here to shoot a brace of pheasant; today, the guns are silent.

The island is terraced with contoured paths leading the visitor through a vast collection of plants and remarkable trees. The azaleas, magnolias, and camellia hedges

ABOVE: *Flowers cascade over an antique wellhead.*
RIGHT: *An ivy-covered staircase leads to the entrance of the villa.*

FOLLOWING: *The lily pond and staircase; above the Piazzale is a camellia hedge.*

are outstanding. Behind the villa is a spectacular Kashmiri cypress, which dominates the lawn. On the waterside is a towering palm, the *Jubaeae spectabilis*, over 125 years old. These trees are each the largest specimen of their kind in Europe.

In the distant past the island was a place of medita-tion. Called Isola di San Vittore, it was acquired in 1501 by Lancellotto Borromeo, who built the villa and laid out the gardens. Later, San Carlo Borromeo came here to preach in its eighth-century chapel. Only in the 1600s did it receive its present name of Isola Madre.

LEFT: *The terraces are linked by shady staircases.*
ABOVE: *A flowering border along the steps to the ferry landing.*

Villa Pallavicino
Stresa

THE GROUNDS OF THE VILLA PALLAVICINO are an odd mélange—zoological park and deep shady zones planted with ancient specimen trees, alternating with open lawns, fields, and formal gardens. The utilitarian enclosures of the zoo, which was created in 1952 as a commercial venture, detract from the unified beauty of the park and the pockets of formal elements.

Within the garden, the lake waters take second place to the rushing stream that cascades down the bosky hillside. Yet at various points the lake below is carefully framed. For instance, a series of bent cypresses form an arch that opens onto the lake, giving a hint of a cloister. Fancy bedding and a gushing fountain add vitality here. On the plateau above the villa is a second formal area, consisting of a large, parterred rose garden with small, rectangular pools and a water channel. Its flavor is French. Wisteria, magnolias, oleanders, azaleas, and rhododendrons all flourish in this area, where peacocks and pheasants stroll along the gravel paths. A marble, balustraded portal stands by the hothouse, beautifully circumscribing a view of the lake. One of the most evocative areas is found just beyond the formal parterre where there is an unpretentious grassy path, scattered with wildflowers and edged by mixed annual borders.

LEFT: *Statue of a mounted horseman and rhododendrons.*   ABOVE: *A portal frames a view of Maggiore.*

LEFT: *The small greenhouse.*
ABOVE: *Cypress arches create windows onto Maggiore.*

FOLLOWING: *A profusion of early autumn blooms.*

The Ligurian-style villa was designed and built in 1855 by a Neapolitan, Ruggero Bonghi. He was a conservative statesman and professor of ancient history, as well as friend to the writer Alessandro Manzoni and the religious philosopher Antonio Rosmini-Serbati, who lived in Stresa. Bonghi sold the villa to the Duke of Vallombrosa, who added to the property and planted many of the trees seen today. The duke, in turn, sold the property to the Pallavicino family in 1862, who further expanded and embellished the park, adding hothouses and over four miles of paths. Today the park comprises 500,000 square feet.

The sequoias found here are among the first planted in Europe. Gingkos, planes, oaks, magnolias, and many varieties of conifers and fruit trees are also featured.

Villa San Remigio

Pallanza

THERE IS A nostalgic quality to the gardens of San Remigio. It is summed up by the inscription found behind the villa, translated from the Italian: "We are Silvio and Sophia della Valle di Casanova. Childhood united us and this garden was born of the dreams that we shared in our youth. We planned it as children, and as man and wife we have created it." It is an elegy to past romantic values: descending from the villa, its terraces are dedicated consecutively to Happiness, Hours, Memories, Sighs, and Melancholy.

Silvio and Sophia were first cousins, descendants of Peter Browne, a British-Irish diplomat who bought the property in 1859, and his neighbor the Marquis Federico della Valle di Casanova, who married Peter's daughter. The original villa was rebuilt in Italian Renaissance style. Sophia died in 1960, aged one hundred, after ensuring that the statues in the garden were registered with the Belle Arti, preventing their dispersal. Since 1977, the state has owned the property, establishing a school on the grounds.

Created in 1883, the garden terraces, their fountains and statuary, remain intact. Some of Sophia's roses still bloom over the walls. This is a traditional axial garden, the villa tightly linked to the garden plan. The water can be viewed only from the top terrace, since the villa is set back from the lake. As one descends to the lower terrace levels, the garden becomes shadier, matching the moods to be evoked. Sophia also planned for the garden to be viewed by moonlight.

The first terrace below the villa is that of Letizia, or Happiness: the theme is ancient Roman, with inscriptions and patterned mosaic niches. Below it is the terrace of The Hours. Here a sundial was placed to "mark the sunny hours, brought on by dawn, which drove away the shadows of night." Statues of the four seasons, by the eighteenth-century sculptor Francesco Rizzi, stand on the upper wall. Beneath are Pluto, Venus, Juno, and Bacchus, attributed to Orazio Marinali. Red and white flowers surround three putti, and a greenhouse for lemon trees is found below on the terrace of Memories. On the terrace of Sospiri, or Sighs, is a theatrical group of Venus in her seashell chariot, driving her seahorses, by the sculptor Riccardo Ripamonte. Parterres of roses are set off by pebbled paths with fleur-de-lis patterns, and niches contain more delightful statues. The final terrace at the bottom is that of Mestizia, or Melancholy. No flowers grow here, only evergreens. Sophia's painting studio and a *nymphaeum* face a statue of Hercules and the Hydra signed by Giovanni Marchiori. Adjacent to the terraces is the small church of San Remigio.

ABOVE: *Venus in her chariot in the Garden of Sighs.*
RIGHT: *A niche in the Garden of Happiness.*

LEFT: *The villa is on the highest level of the garden.*
RIGHT: *Tulips and forget-me-nots.*

Villa Taranto

Pallanza

IN 1930, while traveling between Venice and London, Captain Neil McEacharn read an advertisement in the London *Times* for a villa and extensive gardens on Lake Maggiore. Although he had inherited a castle with established gardens in Scotland, he longed to create his own garden from scratch. Pallanza offered a mild climate, gorgeous scenery, fertile, lime-free soil, and access to irrigation. He bought the property and adjacent lots, amassing about one hundred acres. In the 1930s, labor was inexpensive, so he was able to shift the contours of the land, creating a valley with huge granite blocks brought in from nearby quarries. Eight miles of roads and paths were constructed. Seven miles of irrigation pipes were laid, with a special pump to bring water up from the lake to reservoirs and pools. Terraces were built, fountains installed, and the valley spanned by a tall, graceful, single-arched bridge.

The layout is a combination of park and formal gardens with English lawns spreading around the late nineteenth-century villa. Although the gardens do not touch the shores of the lake, glimpses of the water appear here and there, and the Lepontine Alps, which rise up in the distance, frame the garden vistas.

McEacharn successfully created the equivalent of England's Kew Gardens in Italy. Ninety percent of the plants and trees in the garden were first introduced to Italy here. McEacharn traveled extensively around the world bringing back specimens for his garden. From England he imported many rhododendrons. Before Italian customs regulations became strict about importing plant material, he transplanted an extraordinary collection of plants from the Orient, as well as many specimens from Australia, where he lived for six years during the Second World War. During his absence, the garden was carefully supervised by Henry Cocker, head gardener since 1934. The Germans used the gardens as a transportation storage spot, and the pump to the lake was stolen. After the war, many plants were replaced with the help of Kew Gardens. Since 1936 the Villa Taranto Seed Catalogue has expanded from 367 to over 4,000 items.

Among the thirty thousand different plants in the garden are the spectacular water lilies—*Victoria amazonica* and *Victoria crusiana*—with circular pads that extend up to six feet across.

Captain McEacharn arranged to donate his property to the Italian government before the war, retaining the right to live in it until his death in 1964. By special dispensation, he is buried in a little chapel surrounded by the gardens he created and loved. The villa is used for special meetings of the Italian cabinet. The gardens are run by a private company in consultation with a horticultural school.

Fortino del Cerro
Cerro

LEFT: *Asters and chrysanthemums near the walls of the* fortino.
ABOVE: *Brick steps leading to a long path bordering the lake.*
FOLLOWING: *The private port.*

*I*N THE LATE nineteenth century, Cerro was an Austrian-Italian border town with a small fort by the waterside. This was in great disrepair when the Masini family acquired it in 1935. Rebuilding the fort, they matched the original stone, quarried on the opposite side of Lake Maggiore, and finished it with a drawbridge entrance painted in the yellow and black stripes of Austria. The little port was completed with an enclosing wall and a graceful sweep of steps leading to the garden.

A variety of trees was planted, including beeches, stone pines, and cypresses. Along the shore and leading to the fort are mixed flowerbeds. A small lily pool and a rock garden host appropriate plants, but the glory of this garden is the abundance of hydrangeas. All around the *fortino* are long banks of hydrangeas; in June, these bloom in every color, a magical contrast to the severe curving stone walls of the *fortino*.

LAKE GARDA

OF THE THREE principal lakes, Garda is the largest and wildest, its shores the most untouched. From its base, the shallow waters bordered by vast plains appear to be the open sea. Lake Garda measures thirty-one miles long by twelve miles wide. To the north, the lake's character changes radically; it narrows and deepens to become a fiord. Mountainsides plunge into the waters, and cars must pass through a series of eighty tunnels, bored through the rock by the edge of the lake.

Before 1900, Lake Garda was ignored by tourists. The grand hotels, like those of Maggiore and Como, did not exist here. Apart from the rare palazzo, the villas on Garda are more modest, and their gardens on a correspondingly simpler scale. The gardens also have a different flavor here. Apart from a few that were designed for public viewing, such as

Bettoni and Il Vittoriale, Garda's gardens tend to be intimate. They are more personal, tucked away, invisible from road or lake, with an emphasis on individual plants rather than the overall architectural design. My first introduction to Garda's gardens was at the summer house of Mantuan friends. It was a garden to be lived in: we studied there, ate there, hiked up a winding staircase for panoramic views, and fought our way through underbrush to a little-used gate near the main road, to get to the tiny beach and icy late-September waters. Whenever I return to Lake Garda, I return to this garden.

It is not an outstanding garden, and photographs of it do not appear on these pages, despite a pretty view of the lake from its balustrades. But it is a garden beloved by its

ABOVE: *Torri del Benaco.*
RIGHT: *A street corner in Sirmione.*

OST. TRATTORIA
AL PESCATORE

RISTORANTE
BUFFET
"SALADS"

PIZZERIA
RISTORANTE
ROCCIA.

L'ORIENTE

LEFT: *An old wellhead in the town of Sirmione.*
ABOVE: *Count Guarienti's pet goats and cow.*

BELOW: *Geraniums in a Sirmione windowbox.*

family, with an assortment of plants and trees tended with devotion. It holds many fond memories for me.

Lake Garda was famed for its lemon production. Its hillsides are covered with terraces where they were once cultivated. Between Limone and Gargnano there are still thousands of tall stone piers, which once supported the beams over which protective winter covering for the lemon trees could be spread. Eventually, lemons from southern Italy captured the market; their flavor was superior and they had a longer shipping durability. Nowadays, a few lemons are still grown in ancient lemon houses at Torre di Benaco and Punta San Vigilio. The surrounding Alps, including Monte Baldo and Monte Brione, shelter the lake, creating a climate milder than Nice's despite being on a parallel with Maine. The south-facing slopes of Monte de Gargnano and Salò are rich in unusual plant life. The area around Bardolino is known for its sweet fruit.

Yet the gentle sunny days can be deceptive. The Sovar is a fierce Alpine wind, which creates high waves on the

lake, and despite the presence of hot springs within the lake, it once froze over in 1706.

Lake Garda was known as Lacus Benacus to the Etruscans and Romans. The ancient Romans established military stations at Desenzano and Salò. Impressive ruins of a Roman villa stand at the point of the promontory of Sirmione. The newly elected Emperor Claudius II defeated the Germans at Peschiera, which later saw the meeting of Pope Leo I and Attila the Hun in the fifth century.

Lake Garda was controlled by the Scaligeri of Verona during the tenth and eleventh centuries, followed by the Visconti of Milan, and later by the Venetian republic. The castles rising above the lake at Sirmione, Malcesine, Lazise, Maderno, and Riva were built to enforce that domination and block passage into Italy from northern invaders. Castle Lechi on Isola di Garda was the scene of plots to rid Italy of Austrian rule. Until 1918 the northern end of Lake Garda remained Austrian territory.

In 1438 the Venetians launched a mind-boggling operation to block Milanese encroachment. Six galleons and twenty-five assorted smaller war craft were hauled by two thousand oxen across the mountains to be launched at Torbole. As it happened, the effort was unnecessary; by the time the boats were in the water the Milanese had blocked the fleet in the harbor.

There is an inaccessible garden at the Palazzo Martinengo at Salò, behind the walls of a forbidding, massive sixteenth-century building. In 1585, it hid Vittoria Accoramboni, the beautiful second wife of Paolo Giordano, duke of Bracciano, both of whom murdered their respective former spouses. Paolo Giordano was head of the rich, powerful Orsini family. When he died he left his entire estate to Vittoria, to the outrage of his relatives, who stormed the palazzo, forcing her to flee. Tracked down in Padua, she was murdered by her brother-in-law. She was John Webster's White Devil, in his play produced in 1612. The garden, with its gloomy cypresses, cedar, and fountains was described in a letter by Lady Mary Wortley

Montagu in the following century.

Lake Garda has been extolled in poetry by Virgil, Catullus, Horace, Dante, and Giosuè Carducci. Goethe

An olive grove at the Baia delle Sirene.

first approached Italy by Lake Garda's shores, which triggered his lasting love affair with this country.

Villa Bettoni

Bogliaco

LEFT: *Ramp-like steps linking the levels of the* limonaia.
ABOVE: *The perspective staircase.*

*T*HE ROAD TO Bogliaco is narrow, snaking through fishing villages along Garda's western coast. Suddenly, one drives between an imposing palace and curving garden gates, which guard an expanse of formal, wedge-shaped parterres of low box. At the rear looms a perspective staircase. Freshly restored in peach-and-cream colors, the staircase, with its grotto, niches, and ramps, serves to focus the garden and link it with the palace opposite. Flanking it are stone piers of the old lemon greenhouses, now turned into vegetable plots. The palace *piano nobile* is joined by flying bridges across the main road to the garden itself. The original plan called for the *limonaia's* top terraces to lead beyond a small fountain, into the groves of olives on the hillside, to a temple. The Villa Bettoni also has a terrace garden strip along the waterfront. Here are the flowerbeds missing from the *limonaia* perspective garden.

Although the Counts Bettoni had owned the property since the fifteenth century, the villa and garden seen today were commissioned in the eighteenth century by Count Giovanni Antonio Bettoni. He was commander of cavalry for Empress Maria Teresa of Austria. The villa had two architects: the first, Adriano Cristofoli, had a falling-

ABOVE: *Villa Bettoni's lakeside facade.*
RIGHT: *The* limonaias *are still in use.*

FOLLOWING: *View of the parterre from the perspective staircase.*

out with his patron by 1751; five years later, work was resumed by Antonio Marchetti. The garden perspective is the work of the Genoese architect Amerigo Vincenzo Pierallini and dates from 1764. Its niches and walls are adorned with sculpture by Giovan Battista Locatelli.

The garden perspective of Villa Bettoni holds a unique place among Lake Garda's gardens for its concept and scale.

Grand Hotel Villa Cortine

Sirmione

UNLIKE MANY VILLAS that have been transformed into hotels, Villa Cortine has kept its garden largely intact through time. The villa and its park are set apart from the rest of the Sirmione peninsula by two factors: the steeply rising terrain, and the encircling thick curtain of trees, planted, it is said, to shelter an ailing lady from the eyes of the curious local population. The lady in question, suffering from tuberculosis, was probably the wife of Kurt von Koseritz, minister of the Duchy of Hanhalt. Von Koseritz had the neoclassic villa built between 1900 and 1901. In the First World War, Germany became Italy's enemy, and he was forced to repatriate. The property was confiscated by the Italian government at the end of the war. The industrialist Giuseppe Donagemma purchased it, enlarging the villa. Many of the garden ornaments date from his ownership.

The entrance allée terminates at the large basin of Neptune. The sculpture group, with Neptune plunging his trident, surrounded by tritons, is by a sculptor from Vicenza. The moss-covered figures emerging from the shadowy ferns and splashing water are brightened in spring by a front border of tulips. Behind the water theater—an architectural setting for fountains—are

ABOVE: *A river god.*
RIGHT: *Figures from the Neptune fountain.*
FOLLOWING: *Garden paths adjacent to the villa.*

balustrades and pyramids. The hillside rises sharply, with a belvedere part way up.

This natural defensive site attracted the Romans, who built a fort here, hence the name Villa Cortine—a corruption of the Latin word *cortes* for fortress. Its strategic value consisted of surveillance of water traffic and the plains beyond the shores. Later in the eighth century, a Lombard nunnery, Santa Giulia, was established here. The tranquility necessary for a religious contemplative life was often disrupted by bellicose events, forcing the establishment to be disbanded. No original traces of these earlier inhabitants of the garden site remain, but Donagemma collected copies of ancient statues, columns, and inscriptions, sprinkling them liberally in his garden. A scaled-down copy of Giambologna's Pratolino Appennino statue is here, renamed Monte Baldo. Fountains dedicated to Narcissus, Leda and the Swan, and Sirmione appear along the shady paths. Annuals fill the flowerbeds and cyclamen grows wild on the rocky banks. Grand old cypresses, stone pines, and rows of *Trachycarpus fortunei* give character to the garden.

In 1939, Donagemma turned the property over to the Counts Galletti di Sant'Ippolito. They in turn sold the Villa Cortine to Franco Signori, who transformed it into a luxury hotel.

Giardino sul Lago
Sirmione

THIS MODERN PRIVATE GARDEN is the object of great devotion. It is tended with enormous pride and care. It has as neighbors buildings of great antiquity; the Romanesque church of San Pietro in Mavino, and the ruins of an elaborate Roman villa, thought to have been the home of Catullus.

Created after the Second World War on a rugged site, the garden is now at its full maturity. The shores of Lake Garda lie one hundred feet below the rear lawn of the villa. What was once a terraced olive grove, rising at ten-foot intervals, was filled-in with earth, sloping gradually upward to street level. Trunks of olive trees were partially buried and flowerbeds created at their bases. Most of the flowers are annuals, grown on the premises from seeds and cuttings. Two thousand pansies are put in beds at the end of October. These last until mid-May. From mid-October until mid-November there are forget-me-nots, primulas, and calendulas. In the spring, tulips emerge from amongst the pansies. These are succeeded by eight hundred impatiens plants, and in fall by asters, marigolds, dahlias, verbena, begonias, and ageratum. Sage, dusty miller, santolina, and lavender create contrasting zones of gray-green foliage. *Olea fragrans* floods

ABOVE: *Transformed olive groves.*
RIGHT: *Ancient Roman ruins visible from the garden.*

the garden with perfume in May. The roses are exceptional; over one hundred and fifty varieties are cultivated. Yet, despite the splendor of the roses, one's strongest memory lingers on the olive trees, set like jewels, each surrounded by flowers on velvety lawns.

Villa Brenzone
Punta San Vigilio

LEFT: *The* limonaia *of Villa Brenzone.*
ABOVE: *Detail of a property map showing the villa, port, and Circle of Caesars.*

THE PUNTA SAN VIGILIO is one of Italy's lesser-known beauty spots. Luckily, this small promontory on Lake Garda is in private hands, with limited access. The original cypress allée, dating from the seventeenth century, leads down to the gate of Villa Brenzone, cutting through ancient olive groves thick with daisies. To the left of the gate, a lane leads down past the *limonaia* to a tiny luxury hotel, founded after World War I by Leonard Walsh, now run by Count Guarienti Brenzone. It stands next to a tiny port. To the right, the lane leads to the Baia delle Sirene, a sparkling little beach with mountains rising up beyond the waters. This is accessible to the public on weekends. The garden of Villa Brenzone remains private.

As Italian gardens go, Villa Brenzone is disjointed in layout. This is in great part due to the irregular site on the tip of the promontory. Portions of the original eighteenth-century garden remain, but the area around the villa, redone in the nineteenth century, has been altered. The importance of the villa's garden lies in its literary connections; it may also have inspired William Kent, the English artist and architect who studied in Italy and was responsible for introducing romantic designs into the for-

ABOVE: *A garden wall overlooking the lake.*　　　RIGHT: *Entrance to the Circle of Caesars.*

mal English landscaping tradition.

Agostino Brenzone was a multifaceted gentleman of the sixteenth century. A letter written by Pietro Aretino in 1546 depicts Brenzone as an orator, magistrate, and serious philosopher. His spirit was described as *"vago e generoso"* ("attractive and generous"). The garden existed at this time, and Aretino portrays it as silent and fascinating. Brenzone wrote a play (now lost) and an essay praising solitude.

Agostino Brenzone bought the land in 1538 from the Benedictine monastery of San Zeno. In the hotel are bird's-eye-view drawings of the property, showing the villa, the circle of the twelve Caesars, the chapel, and the port, dating from December 22, 1788. At that time, Count Agostino Vincenzo di Brenzone added to the land, purchasing olive groves and pastures from the community of Torri del Benaco.

Nineteenth-century guide books frequently mention the garden. In the past, the design focused on paths leading to groves with statues of Adam and Eve, Venus, Nep-

tune wedding the Sea, Apollo, and the twelve emperors. It has a symbolic tomb of Catullus, and a fountain bust of Petrarch, whose eyes shed tears to water the laurel beneath. Inscriptions abound: a quote from Catullus about Lake Garda, Petrach addressing Apollo, and an invitation from Agostino Brenzone to his guests, "Put aside the labors of the city. Remove from you women and all that regards them. Prepare a simple meal. Nourish your soul with the love of things; fill your hands with leafy branches, flowers, and fruit." Also, "Eden gave death, my garden gives life...why marvel, guest? Then there was a treacherous serpent, now there is an enchanted genius."

A large gravel forecourt with flowerbeds of tulips or salvia surrounds the villa. To the left are high cypress hedges, bent in arches, which are clipped in July and August. Cypresses are planted in rows by the water's edge in front of the villa. On either side they form allées sloping down to a niche containing Venus and a dolphin. Here is a tiny "secret" landing cove nestled between trees. Within the courtyard grow jasmine, agave, bougainvillea, lilies,

ABOVE: *The Circle of Caesars.*
RIGHT: *Villa Brenzone from the entrance gate.*

small carnations, snapdragons, and roses. A path leads around the point, past irises to a belvedere and the little church. Fichi d'India and aloe plants cling to the rocks. Climbing steps, alongside a crenellated wall, one passes a Roman altar. The path winds past the lemon house with its wooden beams; the glass is removed in warm weather. The ancient lemon trees are planted in the ground, some reportedly three hundred years old. An elegant relief in Carrara marble of Apollo is set against the wall. The "philosophers circle" of Twelve Caesars is set on a man-made rise, reached by steps between rows of cypress. Each emperor is set in his own niche; some of these are overgrown with roses. The monument is ringed with cypresses. Sir Lawrence Olivier loved to walk here when he stayed at the hotel. Just outside the circle is a small stone inscribed in 1833 to the memory of a faithful dog. The entrance to the *limonaia* is outside the garden; its gate opens off the cobbled lane leading to the church. By the gate is a Latin inscription based on Pliny's description of the properties of a lemon: made of hot and cold, and sweet and bitter, transformed by Venus into an allusion to love.

The garden has long been tended by the gardener, Nino, as his father did before him.

Villa Bernini

Lazise

LAZISE IS A SMALL lakeside town of great character. Its flavor is determined by its medieval walls and broad piazzas. This sense of enclosed space is present in the garden park of Villa Bernini, just outside the city walls.

On the grounds of Villa Bernini are the ruins of the Scaligeri castle, which was built between 1375 and 1381 by Antonio, the last of the ruling house of Verona's Scaligeri. An earlier ninth-century fort, belonging to Cansingorio della Scala, stood on this site. The Visconti of Milan attacked the castle in 1439 and 1440. Under the Venetian republic it was used as the Palazzo del Capitano, but the Venetians burned it when forced to abandon the position during the period of the League of Cambrai. The town of Lazise acquired the castle at the end of the sixteenth century, holding it until it was auctioned off in 1879 to Count Giovanni Battista Buri. Buri contributed to the restoration of the town walls. At present, the park and ruins are owned by Count Giandanese Bernini, who opens the grounds for concerts.

The paths of the park meander through the courtyards of the crenellated castle. Vegetation softens the walls of a brick hothouse set against the ruined castle

ABOVE: *The brick gatehouse.*
RIGHT: *Villa Bernini from Lake Garda.*

wall. In the park, enormous magnolias and a redwood, plane trees, chestnuts, and pines are among the many trees along the waterside. A brook cuts through to the lake. Lawns now cover the former port, which was filled-in in 1878. Bergenia, canna, and hibiscus bloom beneath oleanders and palms. To the south, Sirmione can be seen jutting out into the lake, a reminder of the Scaligeri northern defensive line, in which Villa Bernini's ruined castle played a part.

Villa Idania
Garda

LEFT: *Villa Idania as seen from the lower lawn.*
ABOVE *Spring blossoms.*
FOLLOWING: *The lower lawn seen from the annual border,*

HIGH ABOVE the town of Garda, set among fields of olives and vineyards, is the lovely garden of Villa Idania. A play on the owner's name, the garden of Villa Idania was created for Countess Ida Borletti. At the time, she was married to a Scottish sculptor, Michael Noble (whose work is scattered throughout the grounds), and it was her wish to have an English-style garden. When they bought the property in 1956, the old villa was surrounded by gravel. She persuaded Alec Edwards, the curator of rock gardens at England's Kew Gardens, to design her garden.

He salvaged five pear trees, the cypresses, and a few olive trees around the villa. A magnificent lawn was planted, which thrives on daily watering made possible by an extensive system for pumping water from the lake. The stone risers of the steps leading down to the border garden are invisible from the villa: it appears to be a continuous, sweeping, grassy slope. Edwards created a rock garden and a border intended to be filled only with annuals, contrary to the English custom of favoring perennials. The first year there were four thousand tulips. The garden was further developed under the guidance of Henry Cocker. It covers less than three acres, but it is

201

LEFT: *These risers are invisible from the top of the slope.*

ABOVE: *Idania is located high above Garda, and surrounded by olive groves and vineyards.*

filled with an impressive variety of prized specimen trees, carefully selected for their contrasting shapes and shades. A lotus pool, and an exquisite arbor bordered by flowering stone walls, are special features. To the southwest is a distant view of the lake below. Opposite, vineyards producing Bardolino wine stretch up the steep, rising hills.

Giardino Hruska
Gardone Riviera

LEFT: *The artificially created "Dolomite" ridge.*
ABOVE: *The cactus garden.*

DOCTOR ARTURO HRUSKA was by profession a dentist (numbering among his patients a Russian czar), but by dedication a botanist, who traveled far and wide collecting specimens in Lapland, the United States, Russia, and central Africa. He was attracted to Lake Garda, but yearned for an alpine garden. Purchasing adjacent terraced olive orchards at Gardone, he began to construct his garden between 1912 and 1914. The obstacles were formidable— dry summers, severe winters, and the lack of available irrigation. He linked distant reservoirs by canals and pipes to bring water to the garden; this water flows through the grounds in artificial streams and cascades of miniature waterfalls from the rocky peaks, collecting in small lily ponds. Within this small garden are tropical damp groves with beds of succulents, open lawns near the villa (which is concealed by carefully planted shrubbery), and a series of three mountain ridges for alpine plants.

Entering the garden, there is a clearing with flowerbeds filled in spring with calendula, baby's breath, and Johnny jump-ups. The path leads into a shady grove traversed by a stream. Here are fuchsia and *Cedrus deodara*. Emerging from the shadows, one comes to a

Left and Above: *Poppies and other spring blossoms at Hruska.*

Japanese lily pool with papyrus and calla lilies. Following the stream, planted with lady's mantle begonias, columbine, and purple primulas, one reaches the "Dolomite" ridge. Here, Doctor Hruska built moisture-trapping, steep hills of porous tufa, covered with red Verona rocks, filling the crevices with humus; little waterfalls cascade from their peaks. All the vegetation was carefully planted according to light and moisture requirements. In May the "mountains" are carpeted with a vast variety of blooming plants; rhododendrons, irises, and dark blue columbine grow around the bases of the three rock out-croppings. *Iberis saxatilis* and *Dianthus alpinnus*, which normally grow at an altitude of over a mile, thrive here. Conifers enhance the illusion of the recreated Dolomite peaks. Further along is an open, irregularly shaped lawn at the upper end of the garden, with a cactus collection and a stream cutting across the grass. A grove is planted with ferns and *Phyllostachys bambusa* from India. Two grotesque bronze heads spit alternately across the path. By the aviary near the villa are tree peonies and lemon trees planted in the ground.

The greenhouses and the garden are still supervised by Hruska's long-time gardener, Angiolino Amati, and his family. Since 1950, the garden has been open to the public. Doctor Hruska died in 1971, but his heirs kept the garden going until 1989, when they sold it to an Austrian, André Heller. Fortunately, the new owner cares for its perpetuation.

Right: *Calla lilies and water lilies.*

LEFT: *The Fontana del Delfino.*

Il Vittoriale
Gardone Riviera

GABRIELE D'ANNUNZIO, poet, patriot, playwright, and novelist, created Il Vittoriale for his residence and to preserve his name for posterity. Monuments and garden architecture cannot be untangled here. The garden reflects the then-current Fascist fashion for massive, stark, and pompous statement. Inscriptions are everywhere. The entrance gates open on a courtyard dedicated to the memory of Piave. The River Piave formed the line of resistance of the Italian army between November 1917 and October 1918. A large, open-air theater constructed for performances of his works and concerts overlooks the distant lake, recalling ancient Greek theater sites at Segesta and Taormina in Sicily. Indeed, the entire garden is pure theater. Around the villa, which was named The Priory, are further walled courtyards with inscribed walls, fountains, and a flagpole circled with heads of barbarians. Oleanders, magnolias, rows of cypresses, and groves of olives cover the hillsides. A stream "Acqua Pazza" (crazy water) runs down the steep sloping hill through dense shade. There are three formal garden areas: one, closed off, is found amid cypresses next to the Sciltan Museum; one is by the side of the villa with curving steps and flowerbeds; and upon the hillside on the path to D'Annunzio's mausoleum is a gloomy terrace with an elliptical basin and the Fontana del Delfino. Surrounded by tall, dark cypresses, this fountain with multiple jets features a statue of a girl with a dolphin. When the wind shifts the cypresses, light flickers across the figures bringing this somber corner alive. Garden paths cut through the olive groves and the cypress allée, leading to the prow of *The Puglia*, which D'Annunzio had commanded, now set surrealistically against the hillside. Two streams meet at the bottom of the property to feed a violin-shaped pool, built for ballet performances.

D'Annunzio bought a farmhouse on this site in 1921. Together with the architect Giancarlo Moroni, he planned the villa and library, and the layout of the monuments over the hills of Cargnacco above the town of Gardone Riviera. Although he continued to live here until 1938, he presented Il Vittoriale to the Italian government in 1930.

RIGHT: *Lake Garda from the mausoleum; olive groves and dark cypresses define the hillside.*

LEFT AND ABOVE: *The Vittoriale is a collection of build-*
ings and monuments linked by courtyards and staircases.

Acknowledgments

In memory of Sherwood Clarke Chatfield and Adolfo Sissa at Bogliaco, Lake Garda, 1970.

With special thanks to Sarah Burns, for her patience, humor, and sharp vision in editing this third garden book for me at Rizzoli; to Liberto Perugi and his wife Mariuccia who spent many a rainy day on the lakes with me; to Mary McBride for her efforts in designing this volume; to Patrick McCrea for all his assistance and enthusiasm for this project; to Roswitha Otto and Cassandra Maresi for their unstinting hospitality; to the libraries of the Kunsthistorisches Institut in Florence and the Hotchkiss Library of Sharon; to Mother Jerome for her continuing prayers; to Le Groupe for their support; to Lilliana Ruspini Schwerin for her suggestions; to Count Giandanese Bernini; Elisa Provasoli Sissa; Countess Maria Bettoni Cazzago; Count Vittorio Bettoni; Count Guglielmo Guarienti di Brenzone; Michele Canepa; Pauline Ames Plimpton; Mackie Davis; Countess Ida Borletti; Marco Magnifico of FAI; Amministrazione Villa Vigoni; Fondazione Konrad Adenauer; Direzione Hotel Villa d'Este; Francis S. Sutton, acting director of the Fondazione Rockefeller; Avvocato Luigi Zagnoli; Raimonda Sanna; Gian Paolo Lodigiani; Giuseppe Spinelli, manager of the Grand Hotel Villa Serbelloni; Countess Sola Cabiati; Baron Pier Fausto Bagatti-Valsecchi; Michele Ferrier; and Signora Masini.

Bibliography

Agnelli, Marella. *Gardens of the Italian Villas*. New York: Rizzoli, 1987.

Ames, General Butler. *Butler Ames and the Villa Balbianello.* Compiled by Pauline Ames Plimpton, Oakes and Sarah Plimpton, Robert O. Paxton. Latham, New York: British American Publishing, 1991.

Attlee, Helena, and Alex Ramsay. *Italian Gardens.* London: Robertson McCarta, Ltd., 1989.

Bagot, Richard. *The Lakes of Northern Italy.* Leipzig: B. Tauchnitz, 1908.

Bascapé, Giacomo. *Ville e parchi del Lago di Como.* Como, 1966.

Batcheller, Tryphosa Bates. *Italian Castles and Country Seats.* London: Longmans, Green, & Co., 1911.

Bazzetta de Vemenia, Nino. *Guida della città e del Lago di Como.* Borgovico, 1924.

Binda, Giorgio. *Romantico Lago Maggiore.* Stresa: Paulon, 1990.

Boccardi, Renzo. "San Remigio." In *Emporium*, 139–40. N.p., 1913.

———. *Il Lago Maggiore.* Bergamo: Istituto Italiano delle Arti Grafiche, 1931.

Borsi, Franco, and Geno Pampaloni. *Ville e giardini.* Novara: Istituto Geografico de Agostini, 1984.

Brenna, Gian Giuseppe. *Tremezzina.* Como: Cairoli, 1969.

Brivio, Dino. *Itinerari Lecchesi—Lungo quel Ramo.* Banca Popolare di Lecco, Lecco: Grafiche Steanoni, 1985.

Burnet, Gilbert. *Some letters containing an account of what seemed most remarkable in Switzerland, Italy, etc.* 1686. Reprint. University of New Hampshire: Scholar Press, 1972.

Castelli basiliche e ville: tesori architettonici lariani. Como: La Provincia, n.d.

Chierichetti, Sandro. *Guide to the Botanical Gardens of Villa Taranto.* Laveno: Reggiori, 1985.

———. *Lake Como.* Milan: A. Preda, 1980.

———. *Lake Maggiore.* Milan: Editrice Preda Abele e A.L., 1979.

Coats, Peter. *Gardens of the World.* New York: Hamlyn, 1968.

Cocozza Tallia, Maria, Vittorio Marzi, Antonio Ventrelli, and Damiano Ventrelli. *Giardini d'arte.* Bologna: Edagricole, 1986.

Como: Le Cento Città d'Italia Illustrate. Milan: Sonzogno, ca. 1920.

Dal Re, Marcantonio. *Ville di delizia o siano palagi camparecci nello stato di Milano.* Edited by Pier Fausto Bagatti Valsecchi, 1726. Reprint. Milan: Il Polifilo, 1963.

Dami, Luigi. *The Italian Garden.* New York: Brentano, 1925.

De' Medici, Lorenza. *The Renaissance of Italian Gardens.* New York: Fawcett Columbine, 1990.

Elgood, George. *Italian Gardens.* London: Longmans, Green, & Co., 1907.

Faccini, Mario. *Guida ai giardini d'Italia.* Milan: Ottaviano, 1983.

Fauré, Gabriel. *The Italian Lakes.* London: Nicholas Kaye, 1958.

Ferrario, Carlo. *Villas and Gardens of the Center of the Lake of Como.* Como: Brunner, 1978.

Fioranti, Camillo. *Giardini d'Italia.* Rome: Mediterranée, 1960.

Fraschini, Marco. *Villa Pallavicino Stresa.* Veniano: Fotoselex, 1981.

Gerli, Domitilla. *Lario Acque Dorate.* Como: Pifferi, 1988.

Gromont, Georges. *Jardins d'Italie.* Paris: A. Vincent, 1902.

Guida di Como e dintorni. Como: Frico Piadeni, 1927.

L'idea del lago: un paesaggio redefinito 1861/1914. Como, Villa Olmo, Milan: Gabriele Mazzotta Editore, 1984.

Isola Madre, Lago Maggiore. Cittiglio: Reggiori, n.d.

Lago Maggiore, Arona, Pallanza, Laveno: Le cento Città d'Italia Illustrate. Milan: Casa Editrice Sonzogno, ca. 1920.

Lake Maggiore with the Borromee isles. Milan: Muzio, n.d.

Le Blond, Elizabeth Alice Frances Hawkins-Whitshed. *The Old Gardens of Italy, how to visit them.* London: J. Lane, 1912.

Lodari, Carola. *Villa Taranto, il giardino del Capitano McEacharn.* Umberto Allemandi & Co., 1991.

Mader, Gunter, and Laila G. Neubert-Mader. *Giardini all'Italiana.* Milan: Rizzoli, 1987.

Mariano, Emilio. *Il Vittoriale degli Italiani*. Verona: Mondadori, n.d.

Masson, Georgina. *Italian Gardens*. New York: Harry N. Abrams, 1961.

McCrackan, W. D. *The Italian Lakes*. Boston: L. C. Page, 1907.

McGuire, Frances Margaret (Cheadle). *Gardens of Italy*. New York: Barrows, 1964.

Moretti, Paola. "Armonie Architettoniche," *Realty* (April–June 1989): 14–25.

Morris, Joseph. *The Lake of Como*. London: A. C. Black, ca. 1923.

Nichols, Rose Standish. *Italian Pleasure Gardens*. New York: Dodd Mead & Co., 1928.

Nobile, Bianca Marta. *I Giardini d'Italia*. Bologna: Calderini, 1980.

Ragg, Laura. *Things Seen on the Italian Lakes*. 1925.

Sale, Richard. *The Visitor's Guide to the Italian Lakes*. Edison, N.J.: Hunter Publishing, 1988.

Sanders, Rino. *Villa Vigoni, un ponte verso il futuro*. Menaggio: Attilio Sampietro, 1989.

Shepherd, J. C., and G. A. Jellicoe. *Italian Gardens of the Renaissance*. New York: Charles Scribner's Sons, 1925.

Spark, Muriel, "Gardens: Plotting an Alpine Cliffhanger." *Architectural Digest* (February 1987): 125–29, 156.

Triggs, H. Inigo. *The Art of Garden Design in Italy*. London: Longmans, Green, & Co., 1906.

Uberti, Giansevero. *Guida generale ai laghi subalpini ed alla Brianza*. Milan: Guidoni, 1890.

Valeri, Diego, and Mario de Biasi. *Lago di Garda*. Rome: LEA, 1959.

Villa del Balbianello. Milan: Electa, 1990.

Visioni del lago di Garda. Novara: Istituto Geografico de Agostini, 1963.

Walker, John, and Amery Aldrich. *A Guide to Villas and Gardens in Italy for the American Academy in Rome*. Florence, 1938.

Wetzel, Johan Jacob. *Il Lago di Como: voyage pittoresque au Lac de Como*. Introduction by Piero Bianconi. Milan: Il Polifilo, 1972.

Wharton, Edith. *Ville italiane e loro giardini*. Florence: Passigli, 1983.

Index